THE BOOK OF HOURS

A representation of the Linnaean Floral Clock by
Ursula Schleicher–Benz.

The Book of Hours

KEVIN JACKSON

Duckworth Overlook
London • New York • Woodstock

First published in the UK in 2007 by
Duckworth Overlook

LONDON
90 93 Cowcross Street, London EC1M 6BF
inquiries@duckworth publishers.co.uk
www.ducknet.co.uk

NEW YORK
The Overlook Press
141 Wooster Street, New York, NY 10012

WOODSTOCK
The Overlook Press
One Overlook Drive, Woodstock, NY 12498
www.overlookpress.com
[for individual orders and bulk sales in the United States,
please contact our Woodstock office]

For Claire

Horas non numero nisi serenas

Contents

Acknowledgements

Gratitude is due to many friends and colleagues, and particularly to: Kate Bolton, Peter Carpenter, Richard Humphreys, Christopher Page, Claire Preston, Rainer Sanger, Peter Straus and Martin Wallen; also to Monty, Mycroft and, of course, P. Wendy Toole was a superb copy-editor, and rescued me from many gaffes. Surviving idiocies are mine, all mine.

Introduction: About Time

'What a devil hast thou to do with the time of day?'
—Prince Hal, taunting Falstaff

1. Clocking On

Sixty seconds to the minute, sixty minutes to the hour, twenty-four hours to the day, seven days to the week, fifty-two weeks to the year ... it is all so familiar, so deeply and comfortably woven into the fabric of our lives, that it is easy to forget that only two of those units, the day and the year, actually correspond to visible operations of the cosmos. All the others we made up, some long ago (our English term 'hour' comes from the Latin *hora*), others quite recently: the word 'minute' entered the language as recently as the 1660s (it was derived from *pars minuta prima*; 'second' comes from *pars minutae secundae*). Traditional, agricultural societies throughout the world have had no need of such precision, and have done perfectly well on a handful of terms signifying dawn, high sun, dusk and deep night.

But city life has always been different from that of the countryside, and modern city life is more different still. Even the simplest cities require some kinds of temporal ordering, and as cities grew ever more complex with the centuries, the technologies and vocabulary of time-keeping grew — by fits and starts — more and more precise. The benefits of mass synchronization have, plainly, been beyond calculation; yet life governed by the clock can be a kind of tyranny, too, as the sacred clowns of the Pueblo Indians were shrewdly pointing out when they began to sport alarm clocks in the dances they performed to mock their white conquerors. However loudly the white men may have claimed that they worshipped only one God, it is behaviour that shows true belief: and any clown could see that the pale-skinned race had given itself up to the worship of strange little machines with moving hands.

The following twenty-four chapters of poems, stories, observations and jokes, though not usually as sardonic as the Pueblo clowns, generally follow their healthy example by stepping back a pace or so from the everyday assumption that our modern, synchronized life is natural rather than artificial. This gathering tries to make some of our common practices seem just a little stranger, and in most cases more complex, than we usually notice. Take, for example, the apparently simple matter of the hours at which we think it right to eat, and the things we consider appropriate to those meals. The large meal that English-speakers call 'dinner' was once consumed at about ten in the morning, then edged forward to what we would now consider lunchtime ('lunch' being, as we shall see, a relative novelty, barely two centuries old), then hopped to the late afternoon (or 'teatime', to cite an even more novel institution) before arriving at its present evening hour of seven, eight, nine or later. As with the hour, so with the edibles: to start one's working day with the once-standard dish of grilled chops and plenty of beer would now seem eccentric, verging on decadent. What we might lazily assume to be a matter of digestion and common sense rapidly proves to be a matter of manners and unconscious assent.

To paraphrase and expand on Ecclesiastes, in our clock-ruled world there is always a due time – usually a remarkably precise time – for eating and a time for fasting, a time for work and a time for play, a time for marriage and a time for executions, a time for formal dress and a time for undress, a time for shopping and a time for banking, a time when you may use profane language or show sexual acts on television, and a time when the pubs finally throw you out. The French, as will be seen, even regulate their adulteries by the clock. In some respects, to be sure, our world of artificial divisions still incorporates the older, 'natural' rhythms of humanity: it makes obvious sense to sleep at night, work – if you need to – in the cool morning, and take a nap when the sun is too hot and too high; and it is a rare soul who has not sometimes felt elated at dawn or melancholy at sunset, or been frightened by noises in the middle of the night.

These few ancient survivals aside, our tacit agreement that pretty much everybody should be doing the same thing at the same time is almost always founded somewhere in history rather than in biology or astronomy. And those histories are often full of unexpected turns. Take the fundamental question of how it is that the strict ordering of our modern day came into being. Historians differ on the point, as it is their job to do. Quite a few, though, have proposed that the hero (or arch-villain) of the tale is one St Benedict of Nursia (c.480– 543). Let's have a brief look at the evidence, and the deep background.

2. From Babylon to Benedict

> The Gods confound the man who first found out
> How to distinguish hours! Confound him, too,
> Who in this place set up a sundial,
> To cut and hack my days so wretchedly
> Into small pieces! When I was a boy,
> My belly was my sundial – one surer,
> Truer, and more exact than any of them.
> This dial told me when 'twas proper time
> To go to dinner, when I ought to eat;
> But nowadays, why even when I have,
> I can't fall to unless the sun gives leave.
> The town's so full of these confounded dials ...

Thus a character in a play attributed to Plautus, *Boeotia*, written around the end of the third century BC. It shows a number of interesting things, one of them being that sundials were still something of a novelty to the Romans of Plautus' day (and Pliny the Elder confirms this, stating that sundials had been introduced to Rome early in the third century). Another is that the business of protesting against 'artificial' time and in favour of 'natural' time is of considerable antiquity. Plautus' character has not thought the matter through deeply enough, though. The technology of the sundial might have been a relative johnny-come-lately, but the Romans – educated Romans, anyway – had always chopped their days and nights into pieces.

Rome, and Greece before it, divided the day into twenty-four fragments, just as we do. They inherited this system from the Babylonians, by means that need not detain us. What the Babylonians had done was to split quotidian experience into the two obvious halves of day and night, and then split those two halves into twelve fractions each. As quick-witted readers will already have noticed, this means that the Babylonian 'hour' – and so the Greek, and Roman, and later the European hour – was not a fixed length; only twice a year, at the equinoxes, were the hours as long as we now know them. The Romans *did* have the concept of equal hours (called either *horae aequinoctales* or *horae aequales*), but only astrologers and speculative thinkers bothered much about them.

For most Romans, it was generally adequate to know that the night was divided into four watches, each one named after its last 'hour', and proclaimed aloud by sentries. If one needed greater accuracy than this, there was a considerable vocabulary of time-words mainly based on degrees of light and dark: *occasus solis* (sunset), *crepusculum* (dusk), *vesperum* (appearance of the evening star), *conticinium* (the falling of silence), *intempestum* (complete cessation of activity), and so on.

Between the dawn of the sundial and the arrival of clockwork, humanity devised a wide range of non-weather-based methods for telling the time. One of the most popular was the *clepsydra* – literally, water-thief – primitive forms of which had appeared in nations from Egypt and Babylon to India and China. Clepsydras measured time by means of the regulated flow of a small stream of liquid from a large, gradated vessel. They seem to have been used by the Egyptians as early as *c.*1500 BC, though it was not until a thousand years later that they came to play a major role in public life – for example, in regulating the length of speeches in Athens's law courts and assemblies.

After clepsydras came more advanced forms of water clock, and slow-burning candles, and hour glasses, and other ingenious contrivances, and for the most part they did their job well enough. Then came the great leap forward: the mechanical clock. It used to be said that the advent of the clock was like a great loss of innocence: suddenly, people became highly self-conscious about the passage of time and all aspects of temporality. More recently, however, this sensible-looking proposition has been turned upside down like an hour glass. As David S. Landes puts it in his study *Revolution in Time: Clocks and the Making of the Modern World* (1983): 'The clock did not create an interest in time measurement; the interest in time measurement led to the invention of the clock.' And this is where we may return to St Benedict.

3. Monks and their Habits

Islam requires the faithful to pray five times a day – at dawn, after noon, before sunset, after sunset, after dark. Judaism requires three daily sets of prayers, also set by the sun and the stars. Christians, too, used to pray in accordance with the movements of the heavens, until the sixth century AD, when someone – guess who? – decided that the system could stand some revisions. The *Rule* of St Benedict, *c.* AD 530, laid down various conditions, which later became a model for many monastic orders. Following the authority of Psalm 119 – 'Seven times a day do I praise thee' – he determined that monks should all pray in unison seven times a day, in services known as Vigils (later called Matins), Lauds, Prime, Tierce or Terce, Sext, None, Vespers and Compline (which, to be pedantic, adds up to eight times, but Matins and Lauds ran together).

The Benedictine rule was widely adopted. Thanks to the ringing of bells, monastic time-keeping was spread across the countryside; punctuality became a new obsession, and constant research into time-keeping mechanisms eventually resulted in the making of the clock. Fittingly, the man most commonly credited with the breakthrough was Canon Gerbert, later Pope Sylvester II (999– 1003), though more cautious accounts say that, while Gerbert probably understood the principle of clock construction, he may well not have put theory into practice. At any rate, it took another three centuries and more before clocks began to appear in belfries and towers. The first true clocks of which we have incontestable evidence are those made by Roger Stoke for Norwich Cathedral (1321– 5), by Richard of Wallingford for St Albans (c.1330– 60) and by Giovanni de'Dondi (1364).

How important was this invention? Very. In his highly influential study of mechanical culture, *Technics and Civilization* (1934), the polymathic Lewis Mumford contended:

> The clock is not merely a means of keeping track of the hours, but of synchronizing the action of men.

> The clock, not the steam-engine, is the key-machine of the modern industrial age ... In its relationship to determinable quantities of energy, to standardization, to automatic action, and finally to its own special product, accurate timing, the clock has been the foremost machine in modern technics; and at each period it has remained in the lead: it marks a perfection toward which other machines aspire.

Mumford is also, one should add, among the leading proponents of the view that the man behind all this is our new friend St Benedict. He points out that although – according to a widely credited legend – it may have been a bull of Pope Sabinianus (AD 605– 6) that declared church bells should be rung loud to mark the passing of the hours of the day, and thus served to regulate for the first time all modes of civil activity, it was St Benedict's imposition of a strict regularity on monastic life that provided the essential foundation for modern time-keeping. Mumford's view, though not uncontested, has not gone unsupported, either. In an essay on feudal society, H. E. Hallam suggests that the search for an accurate mechanical clock was driven 'by the need for the monastery to know the correct time and to be able to measure its lapse'; for Hallam, the 'spirit of the clock' is 'wholly Benedictine'. And in *The Climax of Rome* (1968), Michael Grant proposes that it was Benedict's straitening of the monastic day that made 'western monks into missionaries, explorers, cultivators and preservers of inherited culture'.

Benedict also had a major impact on the book industry.

4. Books of Hours

Asked to name the best-selling book in Europe during the later Middle Ages, most intelligent readers would probably say the Bible. A good guess, but wrong: the mediaeval equivalent of our *Harry Potter* or *Da Vinci Code* smash hits were the Books of Hours, or *Horae*: 'From the late thirteenth to the early sixteenth century, the Book of Hours was *the* mediaeval best-seller, number one for nearly 250 years. More Books of Hours, in manuscript and, at the end of the Middle Ages, in printed editions, were produced during this period than any other type of book, including the Bible' (Roger S. Wieck, *The Book of Hours in Medieval Art and Life*, 1988).

Often magnificently illustrated – so much so that certain *Horae*, notably the *Très riches heures du Duc de Berry,* have remained well known to the present day – these Books of Hours took over the seven canonical hours of St Benedict's Rule and made them available to a pious lay audience, keen to mimic the clergy. The illustrations for each of the hours would correspond to set passages from the Bible. A fine early English example, the de Brailes Hours, has the canonical hours corresponding to Christ's last day:

Matins: The agony in the garden
Lauds: Betrayal
Prime: Christ before Pilate
Terce: Flagellation
Sext: Christ carrying the cross
None: Crucifixion
Vespers: Deposition
Compline: Entombment

In France, Books of Hours more often depicted the life of the Blessed Virgin:

Matins: Annunciation
Lauds: Visitation
Prime: Nativity
Terce: Annunciation to the shepherds
Sext: Adoration of the Magi
None: Presentation in the Temple
Vespers: Flight into Egypt (or Massacre of the Innocents)
Compline: Coronation of the Virgin

Believers and atheists alike continue to derive great pleasure from *Horae*, and they have inspired many other works of art. In the twentieth century, W. H. Auden used them as a source for his most ambitious encyclopaedia–poem 'Horae Canonicae' (sketched 1947, begun 1949, completed 1955), which addresses the twenty-four hours of a single day, the decades of a human life from birth to death, the Rise and Fall of a City, and all of time itself from the Creation to the Last Judgement. As in some of the original *Horae*, it has the Crucifixion at its centre.

It was while reflecting on Auden's sombre poem and on his many prose asides on the subject of time (Auden, who claimed never to feel hungry unless the clock told him to, defined himself as belonging to the species or genus 'Punctual Man') that I developed the idea for this much more modest, light-hearted and (with luck) amusing *Book of Hours*. Instead of the seven hours of the canonical day, I would follow the twenty-four hours of the secular day; instead of offering prayers suitable to each hour, I would gather the poetry, prose, history, sociology, comedy and oddities suited to those divisions. St Benedict would have despised the frivolity, but recognized the form. 'What a devil hast thou to do with the time of day?' A lot more than Hal might have thought, I would reply, for none of us, whether callow Prince or ancient drunk, can wholly escape the rule of the clock. What we can do is use our hours pleasantly or well; and if this particular *Book of Hours* achieves nothing more substantial, I do hope it will prove an agreeable way of passing the time.

KJ
'Moosebank'
5 May 2006

Part One: 6 a.m. to Noon

6 a.m. to 7 a.m.

DAWN

'What,' it will be Question'd, 'When the Sun rises, do you not see a round disc of fire somewhat like a Guinea?' O no, no, I see an Innumerable company of the Heavenly host crying, 'Holy, Holy, Holy is the Lord God Almighty.' I question not my Corporeal or Vegetative Eye any more than I would Question a Window concerning a Sight. I look thro' it & not with it.
—William Blake, *A Vision of the Last Judgment*, c.1810

Composed Upon Westminster Bridge, September 3, 1802

Earth has not anything to show more fair:
Dull would he be of soul who could pass by
A sight so touching in its majesty;
This City now doth, like a garment, wear
The beauty of the morning; silent, bare,
Ships, towers, domes, theatres, and temples lie
Open unto the fields, and to the sky;
All bright and glittering in the smokeless air.
Never did sun more beautifully steep
In his first splendour, valley, rock, or hill;
Ne'er saw I, never felt, a calm so deep!
The river glideth at his own sweet will:
Dear God! the very houses seem asleep;
And all that mighty heart is lying still!
                                        —William Wordsworth

6 a.m. was the original hour of Prime – 'First Hour'.

The Angelus was usually recited for the first of three times at 6 a.m.; it was repeated at noon and 6 p.m. The spacing of the Angelus bell was thus a useful time-keeping device for the lay people of the district.

⊰ ⊱

ON THE AUBADE

Daybreak is one of the few times of day to which a literary genre has been solely devoted. (The evening is another, with its Serenade, or evening song.) The Aubade is a short love poem, supposedly written at dawn, and generally lamenting the fact that the two lovers must bid farewell to the erotic joys of the night and be parted by the new day. It has its origins in classical poetry – Ovid's Amores I, 13 is a fine instance – but was brought to perfection by the troubadours of Provence in the Middle Ages, and by the Minnesingers of Germany. It has been suggested that the form was an ingenious development from the cry of the night watchman, announcing the coming of day. Variants of the short form in English can be found planted in the midst of much longer works, including such masterpieces as Chaucer's Troilus and Criseyde and Shakespeare's Romeo and Juliet.

> But whan the cok, comune astrologer,
> Gan on his brest to bete and after crowe,
> And Lucyfer, the dayes messager,
> Gan for to rise, and out hire bemes throwe,
> And estward roos, to hym that koude it knowe,
> Fortuna Major, that anoon Criseyde,
> With herte soor, to Troilus thus seyde:
>
> 'Myn hertes lif, my trist, and my pleasaunce,
> That I was born, allas, what me is wo,
> That day of us moot make disseveraunce!

For tyme it is to ryse and hennes go,
Or ellis I am lost for evere mo!
O nyght, allas! Why nyltow over us hove,
As long as whan Almena lay by Jove?

'O blake nyght, as folk in bokes rede,
That shapen art by God this world to hide
At certeyn tymes with thi derke wede,
That under that men myghte in reste abide,
Wel oughten bestes pleyn, and folk the chide,
That there as day wyth labour wolde us breste,
That thou thus fleest, and deynest us nought reste.

'Thou doost, allas, to shortly thyn office,
Thou rakle nyght, ther God, maker of kynde,
The, for thyn haste and thyn unkynde vice,
So faste ay to oure hemysphere bynde,
That nevere more under the ground thow wynde!
For now, for thou so hiest out of Troie,
Have I forgon thus hastili my joie!'
—*Troilus and Criseyde*, Book III, ll.1415–42

JULIET:

Wilt thou be gone? It is not yet near day.
It was the nightingale, and not the lark,
That pierced the fearful hollow of thine ear.
Nightly she sings on yond pomegranate tree.
Believe me, love, it was the nightingale.

ROMEO:

It was the lark, the herald of the morn;
No nightingale. Look, love, what envious streaks

Do lace the severing clouds in yonder East.
Night's candles are burnt out, and jocund day
Stands tiptoe on the misty mountaintops.
I must be gone and live, or stay and die.

JULIET:

Yon light is not daylight; I know it, I.
It is some meteor that the sun exhales
To be to thee this night a torchbearer
And light thee on thy way to Mantua.
Therefore stay yet; thou need'st not to be gone.

ROMEO:

Let me be ta'en, let me be put to death.
I am content, so thou wilt have it so.
I'll say yon gray is not the morning's eye,
'Tis but the pale reflex of Cynthia's brow;
Nor that is not the lark whose notes do beat
The vaulty heaven so high above our heads.
I have more care to stay than will to go.
Come, death, and welcome! Juliet wills it so.
How is't my soul? Let's talk; it is not day...
—*Romeo and Juliet*, III.*v*

Perhaps the best-known of all English examples of the pure Aubade
form was written by Donne.

The Sun Rising

Busy old fool, unruly Sun,
Why dost thou thus,
Through windows, and through curtains, call on us?
Must to thy motions lovers' seasons run?

Saucy pedantic wretch, go chide
Late schoolboys, and sour prentices,
Go tell court-huntsmen that the King will ride,
Call country ants to harvest offices;
Love, all alike, no season knows, nor clime,
Nor hours, days, months, which are the rags of time.

Thy beams, so reverend and strong
Why shouldst thou think?
I could eclipse and cloud them with a wink,
But that I would not lose her sight so long:
If her eyes have not blinded thine,
Look, and tomorrow late, tell me
Whether both the Indias of spice and mine
Be where thou leftst them, or lie here with me.
Ask for those Kings whom thou sawst yesterday,
And thou shalt hear: 'All here in one bed lay.'

She is all States, and all Princes I,
Nothing else is:
Princes do but play us; compar'd to this,
All honour's mimic, all wealth alchemy.
Thou, sun, art half as happy as we,
In that the world's contracted thus;
Thine age asks ease, and since thy duties be
To warm the world, that's done in warming us.
Shine here to us, and thou art everywhere;
This bed thy centre is, these walls, thy sphere.
　　　　　　　—John Donne, c.1603 or slightly later

Over the decades and centuries, the Aubade form becomes more and more adaptable for other purposes. By the Victorian period, the tradition has grown capacious enough to be turned into a graver kind of lament at enforced parting in Tennyson's great poem of mourning – here, at morning:

Dark house, by which once more I stand
  Here in the long unlovely street,
  Doors, where my heart was used to beat
So quickly, waiting for a hand,

A hand that can be clasped no more –
  Behold me, for I cannot sleep
  And like a guilty thing I creep
At earliest morning to the door.

He is not here; but far away
  The noise of life begins again
  And ghastly through the drizzling rain
On the bald street breaks the blank day.
          —Tennyson, 'In Memoriam A.H.H.',
                  published 1850

William Empson's 'Aubade' (first published in 1937), a poem written in anticipation of the coming World War, is perhaps the finest twentieth-century example of the form, though Richard Wilbur's more conventional 'A Late Aubade' is probably the most erotic.

❧ ☙

Um Sechse des Morgens ward er gehenkt,
Um Sieben ward er ins Grab gesenkt;
Sie aber schon um Achte
Trank roten Wein und lachte.
          —Heinrich Heine (1797–1856)

['At six in the morning they hanged him, at seven they laid him in the grave; but on the dot of eight, she drank red wine and laughed.']

Six of the clock

It is now the first hour, the sweet time of the morning, and the sun at every window calls the sleepers from their beds: the marigold begins to open her leaves, and the dew on the ground doth sweeten the air: the falconers now meet with many a fair flight, and the hare and the hounds have made the huntsman good sport: the shops in the city begin to shew their wares, and the market people have taken their places: the scholars now have their forms, and whosoever cannot say his lesson must presently look for absolution: the forester now is drawing home to his lodge, and if his deer be gone, he may draw after cold scent: now begins the curst mistress to put her girls to their tasks, and a lazy hylding will do hurt among good workers; now the mower falls to whetting of his scythe, and the beaters of hemp give a ho! to every blow: the ale-knight is at his cup ere he can well see his drink, and the beggar is as nimble-tongued, as if he had been at it all day: the fishermen now are at the crayer for their oysters, and they will never tire crying, while they have one in their basket. In sum, not to be tedious, I hold it the sluggard's shame and the labourer's praise. Farewell.

—Nicholas Breton, *The Fantasticks*, 1626

[hylding: 'hinder-ling', 'base wretch'; crayer: crier]

My own life is — I rise at six or 6.30 — & work a short hour before breakfast at 8. Bkft as slight as possible — 2 cups of tea, 2 bits of dry toast, 2 ditto bacon, work till 11 -; newspaper. Work again until 2. small bit of cake. — work till 4. Dine. simple sole and beneficial beer; work again till 7. wash brushes and swear till 7.30. Prowl in the dark along the melancholy sea till 8.45. Bed at 9.30. For I am too sad and tired by that time to work again. Bed extremely uncomfortable — like a plum pie turned into stone. Lie awake and have the cramp & the side-ache till morning. Then the 'break, break, break' of the sea

gets me to sleep. I have a piano, but seldom play. Housemaid
vexatious & a goose, – wears crinolines.

> —Edward Lear, from St. Leonard's-on-Sea, to Chichester
> Fortesque (Lord Carlingford), 29 August 1861.
> The 'break, break, break' here alludes to
> Tennyson's poem of the same name.

A Whimsical View of Morning:

'Tis the hour when white-horsed Day
Chases Night her mares away,
When the Gates of Dawn (they say)
    Phoebus opes:
And I gather that the Queen
May be uniformly seen,
Should the weather be serene,
    On the slopes.

When the ploughman as he goes
Leathern-gated o'er the snows,
From his hat and from his nose
    Knocks the ice;
And the panes are frosted o'er
And the lawn is crisp and hoar,
As has been observed before
    Once or twice.

When arrayed in breastplate red
Sings the robin, for his bread,
On the elmtree that hath shed
    Every leaf;
While, within, the frost benumbs
The still sleepy schoolboy's thumbs,
And in consequence his sums
    Come to grief.

But when breakfast-time hath come,
And he's crunching crust and crumb
He'll no longer look a glum
    Little dunce;
But be as brisk as bees that settle
On a summer rose's petal:
Wherefore, Polly, put the kettle
    On at once.
              —C. S. Calverley (1831-84)

At 6.20 a.m. on Boxing Day, 1937, a date and time chosen for astro-logical reasons (the sun was moving into Capricorn), the English magus Aleister Crowley – known to the yellow press as 'the wickedest man in the world' – was waiting on the embankment of the river Thames, just by Cleopatra's Needle. With him was a motley, multi-racial crowd: his disciple Gerald Yorke, plus an Indian, a Jew, a Malay and an African, each one of them picked up in the course of an epic pub-crawl the night before. To Crowley's mind, this quartet represented all the principal races of the world. At exactly 6.22, Crowley ceremonially presented them with copies of *The Equinox of the Gods* – an extremely handsome volume, bound in buckram and elaborately embossed with esoteric symbols. It seems that Crowley intended this manifesto to inaugurate a new era for the world. Crowley's randomly collected quartet left quietly; if a New Age had indeed begun, no one noticed.

Twenty-one years earlier, at 6.20 a.m. on 15 September 1916, forty-nine British tanks advanced into the Somme, so launching the first ever armoured assault.

 ⊣⊢

WAKING UP

He looked at the alarm-clock ticking on the chest. Heavenly Father! he thought. It was half past six o'clock and the hands were moving quietly on, it was even past the half-hour, it was getting on for a quarter to seven. Had the alarm-clock not gone off? From the bed one could see that it had been properly set for four o'clock; of course it must have gone off. Yes, but was it possible to sleep quietly through that ear-splitting noise? Well, he had not slept quietly, yet apparently all the more soundly for that. But what was he to do now? The next train went at seven o'clock; to catch that he would have to hurry like mad and his samples weren't even packed up, and he himself wasn't feeling particularly fresh and active. And even if he did catch the train he wouldn't avoid a row with the chief, since the warehouse porter would have been waiting for the five o'clock train and would have long since reported his failure to turn up.

... As all this was running through his mind at top speed without his being able to decide to leave his bed – the alarm-clock had just struck a quarter to seven – there came a cautious tap at the door behind the head of his bed. 'Gregor,' said a voice – it was his mother's – 'it's a quarter to seven. Hadn't you a train to catch?'

—Franz Kafka, *Metamorphosis*, 1916 (trans. Willa and Edwin Muir, 1933)

(Gregor Samsa has turned into an insect overnight. Kafka's tale has attracted countless allegorical interpretations, of which the wittiest came from Kingsley Amis, who suggested that, far from being fantastical, it is a brilliantly realistic account of a hangover.)

7 a.m. to 8 a.m.

Seven of the Clock

Seven of the clock and the day
Clean as a copybook, white
As I go whistling on my way,

Two flying feet
Hopscotch through the street
All the way down
To the end of the town,

O breathless I am and blowing
Like a whale, a spinnaker sail
On a Summer sea,

Feet and fist
Reach out through the mist
For the bridge that grows like a Roman nose
In a landscape as noble as this,

Now over I go but adagio
For this is the slow
Movement of Matins,

See far below
The ballet begins
And I make my bow
To swans on a lake,

O this is the hour when life's begun
To unfold in the flower
Face and hands to the sun,

This is the time for the hare to run
From shouts and shadows and
Shots from a gun,

When the stag in the park
Awoke with a start, antlers
Caught in the arms of an oak,

And everywhere suddenly broke
News of a day, bells and chimes
And the definite stroke

Of Seven of the Clock.
> —Roy Macnab (South African poet,
> journalist and diplomat, b.1923)

When he was an undergraduate, the comic poet Richard Harris Barham – now remembered, if at all, for the *Ingoldsby Legends* (1840) – was carpeted by his tutor for persistent non-attendance at 7 a.m. chapel services. Barham excused himself by saying that this service was 'too late' for him. 'Too late?' 'Yes, sir. I'm a man of regular habits, and I can't sit up until seven o'clock in the morning. Unless I get to bed by four, or five at the latest, I'm good for nothing next day.'

As was customary at the time, Oscar Wilde was released from his imprisonment at Reading Gaol early in the morning. Among the small group of loyal supporters gathered to meet him at the house of a mutual friend was Ada Leverson, affectionately known as 'The Sphinx'. When he saw her, Wilde said, 'Sphinx, how marvellous of you to know exactly the right hat to wear at seven o'clock in the morning to meet a friend who has been away.'

-≼ ≽-

ON BREAKFASTS: A SHORT HISTORY

To our ancestors – the better-off and more leisured ones, anyway – seven o'clock would have seemed quite an early hour at which to break one's nightly fast; but for the hypothetical Regular Joe or Jill of the twenty-first century, someone who has to be at work or in the class or the dole queue by 9 a.m., and often has to endure the better part of an hour on tube or train or bus to meet that glum deadline, 7 a.m. is about the right time to take on the morning's main fuel. Not that we perform that basic function very well nowadays. To the despair of nutritionists, who must by now be weary of shouting from the rooftops that breakfast is by far the most important meal of the day and never, ever to be skipped, most of us barely manage to gulp down more than a slice of toast thinly spread with I-can-easily-believe-it's-not-butter, or a bowl of sweetened cereal with semi-skimmed milk, or a pot of low-fat fruity yoghurt. Quite a few of us settle for a cup of tea or instant coffee; or nothing at all.

They ordered these matters differently in the eighteenth century:

Waverley found Miss Bradwardine presiding over the tea and coffee, the table loaded with warm bread, both of flour, oatmeal and barleymeal, in the shape of loaves, cakes, biscuits, and other varieties, together with eggs, reindeer ham, mutton and beef ditto, smoked salmon, marmalade, and all the other delicacies which induced even Johnson himself to extol the luxury of a Scotch breakfast above that of all other countries. A mess of oatmeal porridge, flanked by a silver jug, which held an equal mixture of cream and milk, was placed for the Baron's share of this repast.

Thus Sir Walter Scott, in *Waverley*; his Johnsonian reference is presumably to a well-known passage in his *Journey to the Western Islands* in which the Great Cham reluctantly admits that:

In the breakfast, the Scots, whether of the Lowlands or mountains, must be confessed to excel us. The tea and coffee are accompanied not only with butter, but with honey, conserves and marmalades. [Note that he does not mention the fish or meat.] If an epicure could remove by a wish in quest of sensual gratification, wherever he had supped, he would breakfast in Scotland.

Johnson's admiration was not unqualified:

In the islands, however, they do what I found it not very easy to endure. They pollute the tea-table by plates piled high with large slices of cheshire cheese, which mingles its less grateful odours with the fragrance of the tea.

Johnson was also mildly taken aback by the Scots habit of early morning toping:

A man of the Hebrides, for of the woman's diet I can give no account, as soon as he appears in the morning, swallows a glass of whisky; yet they are not a drunken race, at least I never was present at much intemperance; but no man is so abstemious as to refuse the morning dram, which they call a skalk.

Nor was Sir Walter purely a theoretical advocate of the Great Scottish Breakfast: he put his knife and fork, so to speak, where his mouth was. According to his biographer, Lockhart:

Breakfast was his chief meal. Before that came, he had gone through the severest part of his day's work ... His plate was always provided, in addition to the usual delicacies of a Scotch breakfast, with some solid article, on which he did most lusty execution – a round of beef – a pasty, such as made Gil Blas's eyes water – or, most welcome of all, a cold sheep's head, the charms of which primitive dainty he has so gallantly defended against the disparaging sneers of Dr Johnson and his bear-leader [viz. James Boswell, Esq.]. A huge brown loaf flanked his elbow, and it was placed on a broad wood trencher that he might cut and come again with the bolder knife ...

There were giants at the table in those days. Taking the long historical view over the past half-millennium or so, it is we and not Sir Walter whose breakfasting habits are the oddity, since by and large the British have liked eating as large a breakfast as their pockets could afford and the market could supply. Children in orphanages might have had to content themselves on thin broth, or gruel, or milk porridge; prisoners were handed a lump of dry bread; and the very poor subsisted on air pie and cold water. Otherwise, the British have traditionally fatted themselves on bacon, beef and beer.

A glimpse into the breakfasting habits of gentlefolk five centuries back can be found in the Ordinances of the Household of the 5th Earl of Northumberland, dated 1512. On so-called Fast days, the Lord and Lady sat down to 'Furste a loif of bred in trenchors, ij manchets, a quart of bere, a quart of wyne, ij pieces of salt fysche, vj baconn'd [baked] herryng, iiij white [pickled] herryng or dysche of sproits [sprats].' On 'Flesche days dayly throwte the Yere', the fishy part of the breakfast was replaced by 'half a chyne of mutton or elles a chyne of beif boiled'. That's more like it.

Morning appetites remained keen after the Tudors. In the earlier part of the seventeenth century, the well-off would breakfast quite early, at around 6 to 7 a.m. Their main foods were cold meats, fish – herrings, both fresh and dried, continued to be a popular dish – and plenty of cheese. These would still be washed down with ale, beer or wine, since the novelty beverages of tea, coffee and chocolate (not in widespread use, anyway, until the later years of the century) were generally taken much later in the day. On New Year's Day 1661 Pepys treated his guests to a breakfast of a 'barrel of oysters, a dish of neats' tongues, and a dish of anchovies, wine of all sorts and Northdowne ale'.

As the eighteenth century progressed, it became fashionable for the landed gentry to breakfast rather later in the day. Breakfast was now postponed until 9 or 10 a.m., and consisted mainly of tea, coffee or chocolate, with rusks or cakes, to be followed at about 11 a.m. with a glass of sherry and a biscuit. Wealthy town dwellers took breakfast a little later still, at about 10 or 11 a.m., and often took bread and butter or toast with their hot drinks. The prosperous sections of the artisan and working classes ate more heartily. In the manner of their forefathers, they remained loyal to beer instead of converting to coffee, and consumed prodigious quantities of cheese as well as the familiar cold meats and bread and butter.

It was in the nineteenth century that the 'traditional English breakfast' as we know and sometimes fantasize about it took shape.

It was an old custom at Headlong Hall to have breakfast ready at eight, and continue it till two; that the various guests might rise at their own hour, breakfast when they came down, and employ the morning as they thought proper, the squire only expecting that they should punctually assemble at dinner. During the whole of this period, the little butler stood sentinel at a side-table near the fire, copiously furnished with all the apparatus of tea, coffee, chocolate, milk, cream, eggs, rolls, toast, muffins, bread, butter, potted beef, cold fowl and partridge, ham, tongue and anchovy. The Reverend Doctor Gaster found himself rather queasy in the morning, therefore preferred breakfasting in bed, on a mug of buttered ale and an anchovy toast. The three philosophers made their appearance at breakfast, and enjoyed les prémices des dépouilles [the first-fruits of the spoils] ...
  —Thomas Love Peacock, *Headlong Hall*, 1816

George Eliot looked back in amusement on the carnivorous ways of the moneyed in *Middlemarch*, written in 1871-2 but set some four decades earlier:

'Have you got nothing else for my breakfast, Pritchard?' said Fred, to the servant who brought in coffee and buttered toast; while he walked around surveying the ham, potted beef, and other cold remnants, with an air of silent rejection, and polite forbearance from signs of disgust.
'Should you like eggs, sir?'
'Eggs, no! Bring me a grilled bone.'
'Really, Fred,' said Rosamond when the servant had left the room, 'if you must have hot things for breakfast, I wish you would come down earlier. You get up at six to go out hunting. I cannot understand why you find it so difficult to get up on other mornings.'

'That is your want of understanding. Rosy, I can get up to go hunting because I like it.'

'What would you think of me if I came down two hours after everyone else and ordered grilled bone?'

'I should think you were an uncommonly fast young lady,' said Fred, eating his toast with the utmost composure.

'I cannot see why brothers are to make themselves disagreeable, any more than sisters.'

'I don't make myself disagreeable; it is you who find me so. Disagreeable is a word that describes your feelings and not my actions.'

'I think it describes the smell of grilled bone.'

Unlike Fred Vincy, some of the upper classes continued to browse daintily on coffee and rolls, while some of the rustics stayed true to their beer, beef and bread. Still, a popular household manual of the day, *The Family Oracle of Health* (published in 1824), was closer to eighteenth-century habits than to those of the coming Victorian era. This was the morning diet it recommended to young ladies in search of perfect beauty:

> The ... breakfast itself – not later than eight o'clock – ought, in rigid training, to consist of plain biscuit (not bread), broiled beef steaks or mutton chops, under-done, without any fat, and half a pint of bottled ale – the genuine Scots ale is the best. Our fair readers will not demur at this, when they are told that this was the regular breakfast of Queen Elizabeth, and Lady Jane Grey. But should it be found too strong fare at the commencement, we permit, instead of the ale, one small breakfast cup – not more – of good strong black tea or of coffee – weak tea or coffee is always bad for the nerves as well as the complexion ...

As the Victorian century waxed, Britain's swelling (in at least two senses) middle classes grew ever more accustomed to the substantial three- or four-course meal that still lingers in the popular imagination and can often be found in hotels: porridge; fish (especially the eternal smoked haddock); bacon and eggs; toast and marmalade. This was the standard waking meal in suburban villas, while in grander establishments one could expect to be served with all manner of additional hearty fare, from kedgeree and devilled kidneys to pheasant, mutton chops, roast larks, turbot au gratin, tongue, game pie, galantines, ballotines, brawn and brains. Devotees of Nancy Mitford's novels will recall the occasion when a young man, suffering badly from the previous night's strong potations, totters into breakfast and is confronted with a chafing dish full of hot brains and the would-be tempting invitation: 'Pig's thinkers?'

With such nourishing plenty to inspire them, it is hardly surprising that nineteenth-century novelists should have approached the description of breakfasts with relish:

> ... in the centre stood a magnificent uncut ham, with a great quarten loaf on one side and a huge Bologna sausage on the other; besides these there were nine eggs, two pyramids of muffins, and a great deal of toast, a dozen ship-biscuits, and half a pork pie, while a dozen kidneys were spluttering on a spit before the fire, and Betsy held a gridiron covered with mutton chops on the top ...

(That happens to be R. S. Surtees, but the foodstuffs might be from any novelist of his time.) And we have it on the unimpeachable authority of Scott himself that the French were no slouches when it came to *petit déjeuner*:

> 'There was a *Pâté de Périgord*, over which a gastronome would have wished to live and die, like Homer's lotus-eaters, forgetful of kin, native country, and all social obligations whatever ... There was a decent ragoût, with just that *petit point d'ail* which Gascons love and Scottishmen do not hate. There was, besides, a delicate ham, which had once supported a noble wild boar in the neighbouring wood of Montrichard. There was the most exqui-

site white bread, made into little round loaves called boules
(whence the bakers took their French name of *boulangers*) of
which the crust was so inviting that, even with water alone, it
would have been a delicacy. But the water was not alone, for
there was a flask of leather called a *boittrine*, which contained
almost a quart of exquisite vin de Beaulne ...'

—*Quentin Durward*, 1823

It is rare to find quite such naked exultation over a hearty breakfast
table in serious modern writing – perhaps because novelists, though
they don't usually have to commute to work, share the slender matutinal appetite of our times. That is not to say that there are no memorable
breakfast scenes in modern literature, but rather that modern writers
tend to exult in nuance and peculiarity rather than sheer abundance:
Leopold Bloom's fried kidney in *Ulysses*, the banana breakfast in Pyn-
chon's *Gravity's Rainbow* or the hideous, dyspepsia-inducing
confections, washed down by pints of strong tea, that the poet F. X.
Enderby inflicts on himself in Anthony Burgess's *Enderby* tetralogy. My
own proposal for the modern laureate of the breakfast treat is Kyril
Bonfiglioli, in various passages from *The Mortdecai Trilogy* ... but eight
o'clock approaches fast, and the rush hour is almost with us.

P.S. A Venetian Breakfast:

Begin with a Vermouth Amaro in lieu of a cocktail. For h
d'oeuvre, have some small crabs cold, mashed up with sauce
tartare and a slice or two of prosciutto crudo (raw ham), cut as
thin as cigarette paper. After this a steaming risotto with scampi
(somewhat resembling giant prawns), some cutlets done in the
Bologna style, a thin slice of ham on top and hot Parmesan and
grated white truffles and fegato alla veneziana complete the repast
except for a slice of strachino cheese. A bottle of Val Policella is
exactly suited to this kind of repast and a glass of fine Champagne
and of ruby-coloured Alkermes for the lady, if your wife accom-
panies you, make a good ending. The Maître d'Hôtel will be

interested in you directly he finds that you know how a man should breakfast.

—Algernon Bastard and Lt-Col. Newnham-Davis,
The Gourmet's Guide to Europe, 1903

-⊰ ⊱-

The daily routine of the philosopher Thomas Hobbes (1588–1679; chiefly remembered as the author of *Leviathan*, 1651):

He rose about seaven, had his breakefast of Bread and Butter; and tooke his walke, meditating till ten; then he did putt downe the minutes of his thoughts, which he penned in the afternoon. He thought much and with excellent method and stedinesse, which made him seldom make a False step.

He had an inch thick board about 16 inches square, whereon paper was pasted. On this board he drew his lines (schemes). When a line came into his head, he would, as he was walking, take a rude Memorandum of it, to preserve it in his memory till he came to his chamber. He was never idle; his thoughts were always working.

His dinner was provided for him exactly by elevean, for he could not now stay till his Lord's howre – *scil*. about two: that his stomach could not beare.

After dinner he took a pipe of tobacco, and then threw himself immediately on his bed, with his band off, and slept (took a nap of about halfe an howre).

In the afternoon he penned his morning Thoughts.

Besides his dyly Walking, he did twice or thrice a yeare play at Tennis (at about 75 he did it) then went to bed there and was well rubbed. This he did believe would make him live two or three years the longer.

In the countrey, for want of a tennis-court, he would walke

up-hill and downe-hill in the parke, till he was in a great sweat, and then give the servant some money to rubbe him.

He had alwayes bookes of prick-song lyeing on his table: which at night, when he was abed, and the dores made fast, and was sure nobody heard him, he sang aloud (not that he had a very good voice) but for his health's Sake: he did beleeve it did his Lunges good, and conduced much to prolong his life.'

—John Aubrey, *Brief Lives*, written c.1660s–80s

The eccentric composer Erik Satie once gave a charming account of his daily timetable:

> I rise: at 07.18. Inspired: from 10.23 to 11.47. I lunch at 12.11 and leave the table at 12.14.
>
> Constitutional ride around my estate: from 13.19 to 14.53. Further inspiration: from 15.12 to 16.07.
>
> Various activities (fencing, reflection, immobility, visits, contemplation, dexterity, swimming etc.) from 16.21 to 18.47.
>
> Dinner is served at 19.16 and ends at 19.20. Followed by symphony readings, aloud: from 20.09 to 21.59.
>
> I retire with regularity at 22.37. Once a week, I wake up with a start at 03.19 (on Tuesdays) ...

—Erik Satie, from 'Memoirs of an Amnesiac (Fragments)', in *A Mammal's Notebook*, (trans. Antony Melville, ed. Ornella Volta), 1996; originally published in the *Revue musicale* S.I.M., 15 February 1913

As a young man, the eminent American publisher Robert Bernstein was poached from his radio job by Albert Leventhal of Simon and Schuster. One morning, Leventhal arrived unusually early at the office:

though it was only 7.30 a.m., he discovered Bernstein already hard at work. Bernstein looked up at his new boss and said, 'I'm ambitious. What's your excuse for being here at this unearthly hour?'

-ᴈ ᴇ-

Seven of the clock

It is now the seventh hour, and time begins to set the world hard to work; the milk-maids in their dairy to their butter and their cheese, the ploughmen to their ploughs and their barrows in the field, the scholars to their lessons, the lawyers to their cases, the merchants to their accounts, the shop-men to 'what lack you?' and every trade to his business. Oh 'tis a world to see how life leaps about the limbs of the healthful: none but finds something to do: the wise to study, the strong to labour, the fantastic to make love, the poet to make verses, the player to con his part, and the musician to try his note: every one in his quality and according to his condition, sets himself to some exercise, either of the body or the mind: and therefore since it is a time of much labour and great use, I will thus briefly conclude of it: I hold it the enemy of idleness and employer of industry. Farewell.

—Nicholas Breton, *The Fantasticks*, 1626

Nowadays, 0730 is the hour at which most British prisons begin to serve their inmates with breakfast. Lunch is usually served from 1200 to 1400, and dinner from 1700 to 1930. Eight o'clock has more sinister connotations in the prison world – see below.

8 a.m. to 9 a.m.

KEEPING REGULAR HOURS

The world got up at eight, shaved close at a quarter past, breakfasted at nine, went to the City at ten, came home at half-past five, and dined at seven. Mr Podsnap's notion of the Arts in their integrity might have been stated thus. Literature; large print, respectfully descriptive of getting up at eight, shaving close at a quarter past, breakfasting at nine, going to the City at ten, coming home at half-past five, and dining at seven. Painting and Sculpture: models and portraits representing Professors of getting up at eight, shaving close at a quarter past, breakfasting at nine, going to the City at ten, coming home at half-past five, and dining at seven. Music; a respectable performance (without variations) on stringed and wind instruments, sedately expressive of getting up at eight, shaving close at a quarter past, breakfasting at nine, going to the City at ten, coming home at half-past five, and dining at seven. Nothing else to be permitted to those same vagrants the Arts, on pain of excommunication. Nothing else To Be – anywhere!

—Charles Dickens, *Our Mutual Friend*, Book I,
Chapter XI, 1864

I get up at 8, I walk from 9 to 10; we then breakfast; about 11, I play on the Harpsichord or I draw. 1, I translate, and, 2, walk out again, 3, I generally read, and, 4, we go to dine, after Dinner we play at Backgammon; we drink Tea at 7, and I work or play on the Piano till 10, when we have our little bit of supper and, 11, we go to bed … I think I have very nearly carried another point, which is to breakfast down stairs.

—The fifteen-year-old Maria Josepha Holroyd, daughter of Lord Sheffield, in a letter, 1786

I don't know what you would call a regular life, but I mean by it a life in which one habitually breakfasts at eight.

—Bishop Creighton, February 1871

Undergraduate Tom Brown

We keep very gentlemanly hours. Chapel every morning at eight, and evening at seven. We must attend once a day and twice on Sundays – at least, that's the rule of our college – and be in gates by twelve o'clock at night. Besides which, if you're a decently steady fellow, you ought to dine in hall perhaps four days a week. Hall is at five o'clock. And now you have the sum total. All the rest of the time you may just do what you like with.

—Thomas Hughes, *Tom Brown at Oxford*, 1861

Tom has already explained that his work load is light: '… twelve lectures a week of an hour each – Greek Testament, first book of Herodotus, second Aeneid, and first book of Euclid! There's a treat! Two hours a day; all over by twelve, or one at the latest … '

My Friend, Sir Andrew Freeport, as we were sitting in the Club last Night, gave us an Account of a sober Citizen, who died a few Days since. This man being of greater Consequence in his own Thoughts, than in the Eye of the World, had for some Years past kept a Journal of his Life. Sir Andrew shewed us one Week of it … I shall present my Reader with a faithful Copy of it; after having first informed him, that the Deceased Person had in his Youth been bred to Trade, but finding himself not so well turned for Business, he had for several Years last past lived altogether upon a moderate Annuity.

MONDAY. *Eight a Clock.* I put on my Cloaths and walked into the Parlour.

Nine a Clock, ditto. Tied my Knee-strings, and washed my Hands.

Hours Ten, Eleven and Twelve. Smoaked three Pipes of Virginia.

Read the *Supplement* and *Daily Courant.* Things go ill in the North. Mr Nisby's Opinion thereupon.

One a Clock in the Afternoon. Chid Ralph for mislaying my Tobacco-Box.

Two a Clock. Sat down to Dinner. *Mem.* Too many Plumbs, and no Sewet.

From Three to Four. Took my Afternoon's Nap.

From Four to Six. Walked into the Fields. Wind, S.S.E.

From Six to Ten. At the Club. Mr Nisby's Opinion about the Peace.

Ten a Clock. Went to bed, slept sound.

TUESDAY, BEING HOLLIDAY. Eight a Clock. Rose as usual.

Nine a Clock. Washed Hands and Face, shaved, put on my double soaled Shoes.

Ten, Eleven, Twelve. Took a Walk to Islington.

One. Took a Pot of Mother Cob's Mild.

Between Two and Three. Returned, dined on a Knuckle of Veal and Bacon. *Mem.* Sprouts wanting.

Three. Nap as usual.

From Four to Six. Coffee-house. Read the News. A Dish of Twist. Grand Vizier strangled.

From Six to Ten. At the Club. Mr Nisby's Account of the great Turk.

Ten. Dream of the Grand Vizier. Broken Sleep.

WEDNESDAY. *Eight a Clock.* Tongue of my Shooe Buckle broke. Hands but not Face.

Nine. Paid off the Butchers Bill. *Mem*. To be allowed for the last Leg of Mutton.

Ten, Eleven. At the Coffee-house. More Work in the North. Stranger in a black Wigg asked me how Stocks went.

From Twelve to One. Walked in the fields. Wind to the South.

From One to Two. Smoaked a Pipe and a half.

Two. Dined as usual. Stomach good.

Three. Nap broke by the falling of a Pewter Dish. *Mem*. Cook-maid in Love, and grown careless.

From Four to Six. At the Coffee-house. Advice from Smyrna, that the Grand Vizier was first of all strangled, and afterwards beheaded.

Six a Clock in the Evening. Was half an Hour in the Club before any Body else came. Mr Nisby of Opinion, that the Grand Vizier was not strangled the Sixth Instant.

Ten at Night. Went to Bed. Slept without waking till Nine next Morning.

THURSDAY. *Nine a Clock*. Staid within till Two a Clock for Sir Timothy. Who did not bring me my Annuity according to his Promise.

Two in the Afternoon. Sate down to Dinner. Loss of Appetite. Small Beer sowr. Beef overcorn'd.

Three. Could not take my Nap.

Four and Five. Gave Ralph a Box on the Ear. Turn'd off my Cook-maid. Sent a Message to Sir Timothy. *Mem*. I did not go to the Club to Night. Went to Bed at Nine a Clock.

FRIDAY. Passed the Morning in Meditation upon Sir Timothy, who was with me a Quarter before Twelve.

Twelve a Clock. Bought a new Head to my Cane, and a Tongue to my Buckle. Drank a Glass of Purl to recover Appetite.

Two and Three. Dined, and Slept well.

From Four to Six. Went to the Coffee-house. Met Mr Nisby

there. Smoaked several Pipes. Mr Nisby of opinion that laced Coffee is bad for the Head.

Six a Clock. At the Club as Steward. Sat late.

Twelve a Clock. Went to Bed, dreamt that I drank Small-beer with the Grand Vizier.

SATURDAY. Waked at Eleven, walked in the Fields, Wind N.E.

Twelve. Caught in a Shower.

One in the Afternoon. Returned home, and dryed my self.

Two. Mr Nisby dined with me. First course Marrow-bones, Second Ox Cheek, with a Bottle of Brooks and Hellier.

Three a Clock. Overslept myself.

Six. Went to the Club. Like to have faln into a Gutter. Grand Vizier certainly Dead.

—Joseph Addison, The Spectator, 4 March 1712

⫞ ⫝

Ulysses: Joyce's Book Of Hours

The action of James Joyce's incomparable novel, often said to take place over twenty-four hours, in fact occupies about eighteen hours or thereabouts, depending (a) on what time you think it is when Molly Bloom utters her final drowsy affirmation and falls asleep and (b) how you calculate, or don't, the parts where the narrative jumps back in time from Stephen's morning to Mr Bloom's morning. As the literate world has known since about 1930, when Stuart Gilbert first published *James Joyce's Ulysses – A Study*, Bloomsday (June 16, 1904) runs like this:

TIME	CHAPTER	PLACE/SCENE
8.00 a.m.	Telemachus	The Tower
10.00 a.m.	Nestor	The School
11.00 a.m.	Proteus	The Strand
8.00 a.m. (reprise)	Calypso	The House

10.00 a.m. (reprise)	Lotus–Eaters	The Bath
11.00 a.m. (reprise)	Hades	The Graveyard
12.00 noon	Aeolus	The Newspaper
1.00 p.m.	Lestrygonians	The Lunch
2.00 p.m.	Scylla & Charybdis	The Library
3.00 p.m.	Wandering Rocks	The Streets
4.00 p.m.	Sirens	The Concert Room
5.00 p.m.	Cyclops	The Tavern
8.00 p.m.	Nausicaa	The Rocks
10.00 p.m.	Oxen of the Sun	The Hospital
12.00 midnight	Circe	The Brothel
1.00 a.m.	Eumaeus	The Shelter
2.00 a.m.	Ithaca	The House
After 2.00 a.m.	Penelope	The Bed

⊰ ⊱

The Hiroshima Clock

The clock in the centre of Hiroshima is permanently stuck at 8.15 a.m., the time at which 'Little Boy', the first atomic bomb to be used in warfare, exploded in the air above the town on 6 August 1945.

The Hungarian dramatist Ferenc Molnar was a notorious slugabed, and hardly ever emerged from his sheets before about 1 p.m. When it was demanded of him that he appear in court at 9 a.m. to be a witness in a lawsuit, he issued strict instructions to his servants as to how they should perform the task of dragging him into public at such an ungodly hour. Despite his resistance, they duly had him up, washed, dressed and ready by 8.30, at which point they pushed him out of his front door. Molnar was thunderstruck at the sight of the morning rush-hour – all the workers hurrying down the street – and wondered, 'Good heavens, are ALL these people witnesses in this damn-fool case?'

Miss Havisham's Clocks

All of Miss Havisham's clocks in Satis House are set permanently at 8.40, the time of the morning at which, many years before, she was jilted by her fiancé.

> It was when I stood before her, avoiding her eyes, that I took note of the surrounding objects in detail, and saw that her watch had stopped at twenty minutes to nine, and that a clock in the room had stopped at twenty minutes to nine...
>
> –Charles Dickens, *Great Expectations*, 1860–61

-⋈ ⋈-

Eight of the clock

It is now the eighth hour, and good stomachs are ready for a breakfast: the huntsman now calls in his hounds, and at the fall of the deer the horns go apace: now begin the horses to breathe and the labourer to sweat, and, with quick hands, work rids apace: now the scholars make a charm in the schools and *ergo* keeps astir in many a false argument: now the chapmen fall to furnish the shops, the market people make away with their ware, the tavern-hunters taste of the t'other wine, and the nappy ale makes many a drunken noll: now the thresher begins to fall to his breakfast and eat apace, and work apace rids the corn quickly away: now the piper looks what he hath gotten since day, and the beggar, if he hath hit well, will have a pot of the best: the traveller now begins to water his horse, and, if he were up early, perhaps a bait will do well. The ostler now makes clean his stables, and, if guests come in, he is not without his welcome. In conclusion, for all I find in it, I hold it the mind's travail and the body's toil. Farewell.

Nicholas Breton, *The Fantasticks*, 1626

[nappy: strong, heady; noll: the top of the head, the noddle – hence, a simpleton, or dull drunken peasant]

⊰ ⊱

ON EXECUTION HOURS

Eight O'Clock

He stood, and heard the steeple
Sprinkle the quarters on the morning town.
One, two, three, four, to market place and people
It tossed them down.

Strapped, noosed, nighing his hour,
He stood and counted them and cursed his luck;
And then the clock collected in the tower
Its strength, and struck.
—A. E. Housman, Last Poems, 1922

In Britain, the conventional hours for execution – which, after the decline of drawing and quartering, has usually meant death by hanging – have been in the early morning. (In the United States, the traditional time is one minute past midnight; the favoured methods gas, electricity or fatal injection.) In the eighteenth century, the deadly hour was generally 7 a.m.; in the nineteenth and twentieth centuries, as Housman notes, generally 8 a.m., though executions held in London were, from the early twentieth century onwards, often put back to as late as 9 a.m. Executions have always been a popular entertainment when the crowds have been permitted to watch, and London hoteliers used to lay on a special tourist package which included the so-called Newgate Breakfast, a lavish morning feast. The condemned man may not always have eaten heartily, but the spectators certainly did.

9 a.m. to 10 a.m.

'We shelled the Turks from 9 to 11; and then, being Sunday, had Divine Service.'

—Commander RN to Admiralty, 1915

You get up at 9; sit till 12 in your night-gown; creep down to White's, and spend five hours at table; sleep until you can escape your supper reckoning; and then make two wretches carry you in a chair, with three pints of claret in you, three miles for a shilling.

—Lord Carlisle, on the busy day of a London gentleman in the eighteenth century

Dr John Lightfoot, a Victorian dissenter from the arithmetic rather than the faith of Archbishop Ussher, calculated that the world had been created at nine o'clock in the morning on 23 October 4004 BC. (For a different view, see below, 6 p.m.)

12 March 1391: Geoffrey Chaucer uses his astrolabe to determine the time.

I took the altitude of my sonne, and found that it was 25 degrees and 30 of minutes of heyghte in the bordure on the bak-syde. Tho turnede I myn Astolabie, and by-cause that it was by-forn midday, I turnede my riet, and sette the degree of the sonne, that is to say, the 1 degree of Aries, on the right side of myn Astrolabie, up-on that 25 degrees and 30 minutes of heyghte among myn alminkanteras; tho leide I my label up-on the degree of my sonne, and fond the poynte of my label in the bordure, up-on a capital lettre that is cleped an X; thos rekened I alle the capitalles

lettres fro the lyne of midnight un-to this foreseide lettre X, and
fond that it was 9 of the clokke of the day.'

—From his *Treatise on the Astrolabe*

Nine of the clock

**It is now the ninth hour, and the sun is gotten up well toward
his height, and the sweating traveller begins to feel the burden
of his way: the scholar now falls to conning of his lesson, and
the lawyer at the bar falls to pleading of his case; the soldier now
makes many a weary step in his march, and the amorous court-
ier is almost ready to go out of his chamber: the market now
grows to be full of people, and the shopmen now are in the heat
of the market: the falconers now find it too hot flying, and the
huntsmen begin to grow weary of their sport: the birders now
take in their nets and their rods, and the fishermen send their
fish to the market: the tavern and the ale-house are almost full
of guests, and Westminster and Guild Hall are not without a
word or two on both sides: the carriers now are loading out of
town, and not a letter but must be paid for ere it pass: the crier
now tries the strength of his throat, and the bearward leads his
bear home after his challenge: the players' bills are almost all set
up, and the clerk of the market begins to shew his office. In
sum, in this hour there is much to do, as well in the city, as the
country: and therefore to be short, I will thus make my conclusion: I hold it the toil of wit and the trial of reason. Farewell.**

—Nicholas Breton, *The Fantasticks*, 1626

[bearward: a keeper of bears]

The Konso people of Central Africa number their daylight hours
something like this:

9 a.m. to 11 a.m. *gudada*
11 a.m. to 2 p.m. *guuda'guta*

2 p.m. to 4 p.m. *kalagalla*
4 p.m. to 5 p.m. *harsheda akalgalla*
5 p.m. to 6 p.m. *kakalseema*
6 p.m. to 7 p.m. *dumateta*
7 p.m. to 8 p.m. *shisheeba*

All of these units are indicated by pointing at the place in the sky where the sun would be on that day. Note how the hours become more precise after 4 p.m.: this is because each of the segments is named after the activity that is performed then, and activities increase after the paralysing heat of midday. 'Kakalseema' literally means 'when the cattle return home'.

Nine Ante Meridiem

Those human termitaria, the modern cities, have their own diurnal rhythms. At nine in the morning they have sucked their white-ants, their worker caste of pale-faced, big-headed, small-chested males, and the many females with their immature breasts and pelves, and bodies pallid under their clothes. Only a few belated individuals are seen scurrying to the minute doorways at the bottoms of the skyscrapers. The command that summons them draws away half the adults out of the apartment-cells (which are only the sleeping chambers and nurseries of this social primate). And that command, like the communal will of a true termitarium or ant colony, does not emanate from any central brain or neural plexus. It is not spoken, nor communicated by antennae, since humans have no such useful organs, and it is not even definitively instinctive, which makes it more mysterious even than the directive of other social animals.

So might a philosophic ant write of us, and the complexities of our cities would not baffle her, if we could imagine her with a curious intelligence. At this hour of morning she would impersonally record the flagging *tempo* of the traffic rhythms, and the long flimsy suburban trains being shunted backward now, empty, out of the termini. The beetle-squat ferries are chugging into the bilgy backwaters of our harbours. In thousands of small shops the spiderweb of necessary or pleasurable or titillating objects is spread, and an alert and hungry merchandiser waits at the centre of the wares for the first morning flies. Perhaps the emmet naturalist could comprehend the significance of all this, and of our barracks and our highways, our cattle and house pets, Government doles, mendicants, crèches for working mothers, grain fields and grain elevators. Such things have analogies in her own civilization; so have wine cellars, royal weddings, aeroplanes, perversions of the pleasure-rewarded instincts, even revolutions and communism and predatory nationalism. Certainly she could understand work of a physical sort, for her life is nothing else. Tunnels under rivers, cobweb bridges, even prison quarries and chain gangs building mountain roads would not astonish any ant.

This hour is one of the world's great hours. It commands; it marches with a great tread, and we seldom escape its cadence. No one but a Trappist has time in it for even a hasty prayer, neither does it proffer contemplation or reveal life's deep perspectives, but is instantly all upon us, a column blaring forth the march tunes of duty, which are bad music but catch the legs and set them to tramping. The very birds are at their business, their beaks too full of nesting straws to sing ...

—Donald Culross Peattie, *A Book of Hours*, 1938

᪻ ᪻

ON THE WORKING DAY

'Nine to five' – today, in the anglophone West, a universally understood term for the standard daily hours of work, though the reality is that many people are still forced to endure or able to enjoy much longer sessions of gainful employment. Thanks in part to the catchy pop song by Dolly Parton, the phrase slips as neatly off the tongue as any other well-polished cliché; though, in the United Kingdom, the nine to five,

five-day, forty-hour week only became commonplace as recently as 1950. In 1939, on the eve of war, a forty-four hour week was the standard, and earlier in the century much longer hours were commonplace, especially for domestic staff, shopkeepers and other members of the service industries.

Before the Industrial Revolution, the quotidian hours of work for the bulk of the population were set by the rising and setting of the sun: craftsmen, scholars and accountants managed to stretch out the working hours with candlelight, while the rich – though their pastimes might be remarkably strenuous – seldom did anything that we would call 'work' at all. As noted in my Introduction, the working day as we now know it, organized by the clock, has its origins in European town life during the twelfth and thirteenth centuries. Bells were sounded in the centre of each town, indicating when to begin and end work, calling people to assembly, announcing the start of curfew (*couvre-feu*: 'cover-fire', lights out), and so on.

The advent of better lamps and lanterns, then of piped gas, then electrical lighting, opened up the possibility of working at any hour of the day or night, and it has become something of a commonplace that the working classes and the bourgeoisie alike worked much harder after the development of efficient lighting. Marx thought so, anyway, and later Marxists corroborated his views. The classic text here is E. P. Thompson, 'Time, Work-Discipline and Industrial Capitalism', in *Past and Present*, 38, December 1967. In recent years, Thompson's accuracy has been questioned; but whatever the flaws of his essay may be in detail, it remains likely that – however grim their lot in other ways – members of the old rural population did indeed work fewer hours than their factory-employed heirs. Anthropological studies of traditional peoples support this case: the *Records of the Australian-American Expedition to the Arhheim Land*, 1960, for example, give this gender-based account of the day's work and rest.

ACTIVITY	WOMEN	MEN
Sleeping/lying	9 hours	12 hours
Sitting/talking	8.3 hours	5 hours

Preparing/repairing instruments	–	1 hour
Preparing/cooking kangaroo meat	–	0.3 hours
Collecting other food	4.3 hours	–
Preparing/cooking food	2 hours	–
Singing/dancing	–	1.3 hours
Hunting	–	4 hours

Men thus 'work' about 4.3 hours a day; women about 6.3 hours a day. Nice work if you can get it.

The first wave of the Industrial Revolution in England brought regular working hours of sixteen, seventeen, eighteen hours and even longer, for employees of all ages and both sexes. Humanitarian legislation progressively softened such torments: the first Factory Act of 1819, for example, limited a nine-year-old to twelve hours' work a day, while another Act of 1831 prohibited work by a person under twenty-one between 7.30 p.m. and 5.30 a.m., thus limiting the maximum working day for children and adolescents to fourteen hours. The famous Ten Hours Bill of 1847 only came into effect gradually, and it was not until 1878 that its provisions covered all of Britain's factories. Hours of leisure increased over the next century or so, with far-reaching consequences for all the industrial nations; it is only in quite recent years that the practice of working sixteen, seventeen, eighteen hours and more a day has come to be seen as the exultant privilege of rich entrepreneurs rather than the curse of the downtrodden masses.

So when does 'nine to five' start to seem a fairly accurate indication of the average adult's working day? Quick answer: in the course of the nineteenth century. A few examples ...

In 1800, a tobacconist's in Haymarket printed up a bill of 'Instructions for Staff', which began: 'Open the shop at six o'clock in the Summer and as soon as it is light in the Winter. Cleanse it and put all things in their proper place.' (On her visits to London in 1811 and afterwards, Jane Austen, finding the mid-morning crowds tedious, liked to go shopping at 9 a.m., before her breakfast.) Shops would stay open until dark or, with the increasing availability of the Argand lamp (invented in 1782; see below, 9 p.m.) until nine, ten or later.

In *The Absentee*, by Maria Edgeworth, a senior solicitor is shown to be ready to see his first clients at 11 a.m.; but we also see him interrupted at his breakfast, *c*.9.15 to 9.30, at which time his underlings would already have been at work. In the same novelist's *Ennui*, legal clerks are seen to work from nine to four and again, after a dinner break, from five till ten.

In 1833, Macaulay would take his breakfast at ten (having spent a couple of hours working on his Spanish) and then stroll over to his office, where he would stay until 4 p.m.

The Schedule of Professorial Lectures at Oxford for Lent Term, 1854, indicates that work for undergraduates and their teachers began at 10 a.m. and lasted till 4 p.m., without a break for lunch.

As we have seen, Mr Podsnap thought that 10 a.m. was the proper hour for arrival at his City office, and 5.30 p.m. the correct hour to return home; that was in 1864. But by the 1860s, many offices were open from 9 a.m., even if they were only staffed by junior clerks. In *Nicholas Nickleby* (1838-9), Ralph Nickleby's office hours are 9.30 a.m. to 5 p.m.

By about 1870, the routine for a middle-class or upper-middle-class household was to breakfast at 8 or 8.15 a.m. – punctuality was an increasingly prominent virtue – and the master of the house would set off for work at 8.30 a.m. (As most professional men lived either very near their business premises or upstairs from them, commuting was not much of a strain.) In London, at least, the majority of offices would be open by 9 a.m.; slightly later hours were typical in the provinces. To breakfast much later than 8 a.m. was to be an idler, a Bohemian, and probably a cad into the bargain. The humble work force that sustained this way of life had, it almost goes without saying, much longer hours. A kitchen maid might have to be up and busy by 4.30 a.m., her fellow workers not much later, and even Cook would be at work by 6.45 a.m. To twenty-first-century thinking, these were working conditions not conspicuously superior, on a day to day basis, to those of outright slavery.

In brief, People Like Us have been in the habit of starting work at 9 a.m. for well over 130 years. Futurologists suggest that, whatever other horrors may lie ahead, we can all expect to be working shorter hours (though possibly longer years) from now till Armageddon, but the phrase 'nine to five' seems as tenacious as the still more outdated 'daily bread' or 'Sunday best'. Ms Parton's song won't be needing footnotes for a very long time.

-⊰ ⊱-

In Turkey, on 10 November each year, a minute's silence is observed at 9.05 a.m. in memory of Mustapha Kemal Atatürk, who died at that hour and on that day in 1938.

George Gissing writes (25 January 1888):

A terrible day, got up with a headache, from 9.30 to 2 wrote – or rather struggled to write – achieving not quite two pages. Suffered anguish worse than any I remember in the effort to compose. Ate nothing at 2, but started and walked to Hampstead and back. Head a little better. Dined at a cafe extravagantly spending 1s 9d. At 7 tried to write again, and by 9.30 finished one page.

Mr Pooter is (Untypically) Late for Work

Today was a day of annoyances. I missed the quarter-to-nine 'bus to the City, through having words with the grocer's boy, who for the second time had the impertinence to bring his basket to the hall-door, and had left the marks of his dirty boots on the fresh-cleaned door-steps. He said he had knocked at the side door with his knuckles for a quarter of an hour. I knew Sarah, our servant, could not hear this, as she was upstairs doing the bed-room, so asked the boy why he did not ring the bell? He replied that he did pull the bell, but the handle came off in his hand.

I was half-an-hour late at the office, a thing that has never happened to me before. There has recently been much irregularity in the attendance of the clerks, and Mr Perkupp, our principal, unfortunately chose this very morning to pounce down upon us early. Someone had given the tip to the others. The result was that I was the only one late of the lot. Buckling, one of the senior clerks, was a brick, and I was saved by his intervention. As I passed by Pitt's desk, I heard him remark to his neighbour: 'How disgracefully late some of the head clerks arrive!' This was, of course, meant for me. I treated the observation with silence, simply giving him a look, which unfortunately had the effect of making both of the clerks laugh. Thought afterwards it would have been more dignified if I had pretended not to have heard him at all. Cummings called in the evening, and we played dominoes.

> —George and Weedon Grossmith,
> *The Diary of a Nobody*, 1892

⤜ ⤛

10 a.m. to 11 a.m.

> And then he drew a dial from his poke,
> And, looking on it with lack-lustre eye,
> Says very wisely, 'It is ten o'clock;
> Thus we may see,' quoth he, 'how the world wags:
> 'Tis but an hour since it was nine,
> And after one hour more 'twill be eleven,
> And so from hour to hour we ripe and ripe.
> And so from hour to hour we rot and rot,
> And thereby hangs a tale.'

> —*As You Like It*, II.vii.20-28

From Coleridge's notebooks:

10 Sept 1823. Wednesday morning, 10 o'clock

On the tenth day of September,
Eighteen hundred Twenty Three,
Wednesday morn, and I remember
Ten on the clock the Hour to be
(*The Watch and Clock do both agree*)

An Air that whizzed ... right across the diameter of my Brain, exactly like a Hummel Bee, *alias* Dumbeldore, the gentleman with Rapee Spenser, with bands of Red, and Orange Plush Breeches, close by my ear, at once sharp and burry, right over the summit of Quantock at earliest Dawn just between the Nightingale that I stopt to hear in the Copse at the Foot of Quantock, and the first Sky-Lark that was a Song-Fountain, dashing up and sparkling to the Ear's eye, in full column ...

⊰ ⊱

ON VERY EARLY DINING

It hath been an old Custom in Oxford for the Scholars of all Houses, on Shrovetuesday, to go to Dinner at 10 o'clock (at which time the little Bell called Pan-cake-Bell, rings, or, at least, should ring, at St Maries), and to sup at 4 p.m., and it was always followed in Edmund Hall as long as I have been in Oxford, till Yesterday, when they went to dinner at 12 and supper at Six, nor were there any Fritters at Dinner as there us'd always to be. When laudable old Customs alter, 'tis a sign Learning Dwindles.

—The diary of Thomas Hearne (1678-1735),
27 February (Ash Wednesday) 1723

It was Thomas De Quincey, in an essay mainly devoted to manners in ancient Rome, who gave classic expression to what might be called the First Law of (British) Dinner: that as the years pass, the time at which this meal is taken comes later and later in the day:

In 1700 a large part of London took a meal at two P.M., and another at seven or eight P.M. At present, a large part of London is still doing the very same thing, taking one meal at two, and another at seven or eight. But the names are entirely changed; the two o'clock meal used to be called dinner, whereas at present it is called luncheon; the seven o'clock meal used to be called supper, whereas at present it is called dinner; and in both cases the difference is anything but verbal; it expresses a translation of that main meal on which the day's support rested from mid-day to evening.

Upon reviewing the idea of dinner, we soon perceive that time has little or no connection with it; since, both in England and France, dinner has travelled, like the hand of a clock, through *every* hour between ten A.M. and ten P.M. We have a list, well attested, of every successive hour between these limits having been the known established hour for the royal dinner-table within the last three hundred and fifty years. Time, therefore, vanishes from the problem; it is a quantity regularly exterminated. The true elements of the idea are evidently these: – 1. That dinner is that meal, no matter when taken, which is the principal meal, *i.e.* the meal on which the day's support is thrown. 2. That it is *therefore* the meal of hospitality. 3. That it is the meal (with reference to both Nos 1 and 2) in which animal food predominates. 4. That it is the meal which, upon a necessity arising for the abolition of all *but* one, would naturally offer itself as that one ... '

—'The Casuistry of Roman Meals', 1839

By the middle of the eighteenth century, the moneyed classes had come to a rough consensus that the correct time to sit down for dinner was between three and five in the afternoon, with most families opting for the compromise hour of four o'clock (see below, 4 p.m.).

⊰ ⊱

> From ten to eleven, ate a breakfast for seven;
> From eleven to noon, to begin 'twas too soon;
> From twelve to one, asked 'What's to be done?'
> From one to two, found nothing to do;
> From two to three began to foresee
> That from three to four would be a damned bore.
> —Thomas Love Peacock, 1875

From Oscar Wilde, *An Ideal Husband*, 1895:

LORD CAVERSHAM: Good evening, Lady Chiltern! Has my good-for-nothing young son been here?

LADY CHILTERN: I don't think Lord Goring has arrived yet.

MABEL CHILTERN: Why do you call Lord Goring good-for-nothing?

LORD CAVERSHAM: Because he leads such an idle life.

MABEL CHILTERN: How can you say such a thing? Why, he rides in the Row at ten o'clock in the morning, goes to the Opera three times a week, changes his clothes at least five times a day, and dines out every night of the season. You don't call that leading an idle life, do you?

⊰ ⊱

THE DECIMAL CLOCK

The tenacity of the twelve-hour clock, when all other measurements are inexorably drifting towards decimal systems of measurement, is a curious instance of cultural conservatism. In fact, the Decimal Clock was briefly adopted during the French Revolution, and some of the clocks made in that period still exist and function.

The decree dated Frimare 4 of the Revolutionary year II – that is, 24 November 1793 – divided the day into ten equal parts; each part, though still known as an *heure*, was thus more than twice as long as the traditional, pre-Revolutionary hour. The practical difficulties of implementing this system – which, at the very least, meant either buying new decimal clocks or radically remaking old ones – soon proved so overwhelming that on Fructidor 22, Year XIII (9 September 1803) the decree was repealed.

Incidentally, on the eve of Revolution the French corporation of clockmakers recognised three distinct grades of technician – grossiers, penduliers and menusiers.

-⊰ ⊱-

In 1905, Erik Satie attended the premiere of Debussy's *La Mer*, the first part of which has the sub-title 'From Dawn to Noon on the Sea'. When asked by Debussy what he thought of the new piece, Satie replied that he liked the bit that came at about a quarter to eleven.

Ten of the clock

It is now the tenth hour, and now preparation is to be made for dinner: the trenchers must be scraped and the napkins folded, the salt covered and the knives scoured and the cloth laid, the stools set ready and all for the table: there must be haste in the kitchen for the boiled and the roast, provision in the cellar for wine, ale and beer: the pantler and the butler must be ready in their office, and the usher of the hall must marshal the serving-men: the hawk must be set on the perch, and the dogs put into the kennel, and the guests that come to dinner must be invited against the hour: the scholars now fall to construe and parse, and the lawyer makes his client either a man or a mouse: the chapmen now draw home to their inns, and the shopmen fall to folding up their wares: the ploughman now begins to grow towards home, and the dairy-maid, after her works, falls to cleansing of her vessels: the cook is cutting sops for broth, and

the butler is chipping of loaves for the table: the minstrels begin to go towards the taverns, and the cursed crew visit the vile places. In sum, I thus conclude of it: I hold it the messenger to the stomach and the sprit's recreation. Farewell.

—Nicholas Breton, *The Fantasticks*, 1626

A Day in the Life of an American Slacker, circa 1994

10.52 a.m.	Glorious sleep.
10.53 a.m.	Awaken when you are disturbed by the wheezy breathing of your housemate as he shuffles around in the hallway outside your bedroom.
10.57 a.m.	Fall back to sleep.
11.34 a.m.	Wake up again. Elect to lay in bed awhile longer so you can stare at the ceiling and think.
12.45 p.m.	Plan the world tour you would take if any of your relatives happened to die and handed you a pile of money.
1.33 p.m.	Sit down with a cup of coffee and read the newspaper.
1.48 p.m.	Realize that you write much better than any of the nationally syndicated editorial columnists that appear in your local paper. Wonder how much money they make.
1.52 p.m.	Peruse an op-ed article stating that your generation represents 'the final exhaustion of civilization'. Resolve to fire off a scathing yet piquant rebuttal.
2.00 p.m.	Watch Hogan's Heroes.
2.30 p.m.	Watch second installment of Hogan's Heroes.
2.42 p.m.	Commercial break. Decide to go and work on your newest major project – a flow chart in which you are attempting to categorize and classify every philosopher throughout time according to your very own top-secret rating system – just as soon as you find out how this episode ends.
3.14 p.m.	Leave the house and wander around aimlessly.

3.45 p.m.	Find yourself at a cafe. Get a cup of coffee and set to work on the Chart.
3.48 p.m.	Get momentarily stumped by Schopenhauer. Skip him for the time being and forge to Herbert Spencer.
4.30 p.m.	Show your groundbreaking flowchart to a fellow cafe-goer. Attempt to impress upon him the sheer magnitude of the task you have set yourself.
4.31 p.m.	Shrink back in horror when he blows smoke in your face and says, 'Dude, it's just a list of names.'
4.35 p.m.	Figure maybe you would like to work with your hands. To learn how to make something.
4.37 p.m.	Realize you will be in direct competition with thousands of fleet-fingered peasants from Bangladesh. Your only career options seem to be fifteen minutes of fame or years of manning the frothing machine at Orange Julius.
5.20 p.m.	Return home.
5.27 p.m.	Take a nap.
7.32 p.m.	Get out of bed. 'Borrow' a box of your housemate's Kraft Macaroni and Cheese for dinner.
7.56 p.m.	Resolve to build your own log cabin out in the woods and live off the fat of the land. Begin drawing some preliminary floor plans inside your crisp new notebook.
8.48 p.m.	Hunker down with Schopenhauer.
9.05 p.m.	Partake in shouting match with your housemate over the mysterious disappearance of a box of Kraft Macaroni and Cheese.
9.33 p.m.	Storm out of house, saying, 'Geez, man, I'm not sure I can live with this sort of distrust. Not in my own home.'
9.45 p.m.	Elect to embark on a drinking binge.
9.46 p.m.	Root through your pockets. Come up with seventy three cents and a prodigious clump of lint.
9.48 p.m.	Take a long, reflective walk.
10.13 p.m.	Decide that life's increasing randomness does not let you believe the lies that would make you more normal.

Wish you had a pencil so that you could write this down.

11.05 p.m.	Return home.
11.15 p.m.	Actively ignore the rumblings of your housemate.
11.30 p.m.	Putter around your room.
11.48 p.m.	Rake the sand in your Zen rock garden.
12.15 a.m.	Alphabetize your cassettes.
12.33 a.m.	Practice your dart game.
1.00 a.m.	Assume the fetal position for late night infomercial viewing.
1.26 a.m.	Stare near-crippling bout of existential angst in the face.
1.57 a.m.	Once again, glorious sleep.

—from Sarah Dunn, *The Official Slacker Handbook*, 1994

A cruel caricature of the working routine of Alexander Chancellor, when he was editor of *The Spectator* in the mid 1970s:

10.55 Arrive at Office.
11.00 Lose article by Solzhenitsyn.
11.05 To pub for gin and tonic.

—As reported in Graham Lord's biography of Jeffrey Barnard, *Just the One*, 1992

11.a.m. to Noon

Victorian Journalist George Augustus Sala is Infuriated by 'World Music'

Quiet as I am, I become at Eleven o'Clock in the Morning on every day of the week save Sunday a raving, ranting maniac – a dangerous lunatic, panting with insane desires to do, not only

myself but other people, a mischief, and possessed, less by hallu-
cination than by rabies. For so sure as the clock of St Martin's
strikes eleven, so does my quiet street become a pandemonium
of discordant sounds. My teeth are on edge to think of them. The
'musicianers', whose advent from Clerkenwell and the East-end
of London I darkly hinted at in a preceding chapter, begin to
penetrate through the vaster thoroughfares, and make their hated
appearance at the head of my street. First Italian organ-grinder,
hirsute, sunburnt, and saucy, who grinds airs from the 'Trova-
tore' six times over, follows with a selection from the 'Traviata',
repeated half a dozen times, finishes up with the 'Old Hundredth'
and the 'Postman's Knock', and then begins again. Next, shivering Hindoo, his skin apparently just washed in walnut juice, with
a voluminous turban, dirty white muslin caftan, worsted stockings and hob-nailed shoes, who, followed by two diminutive
brown imps in similar costume, sings a dismal ditty in the Hin-
dostanee language, and beats the tom-tom with fiendish
monotony...

    —George Augustus Sala, *Twice Around the Clock*, 1858-9

Sala was spared this pedestrian concert on Sundays because of the
severity with which the observance of the Lord's Day was enforced by
the law of the realm. On that day, the loudest noise in the streets was
the tolling of church bells, and the most frequently attended service was
the eleven o'clock.

As sardonic observers often noted, the demeanours of Sunday-
Morning worshippers was less then entirely pious; and those who dared
to spend their Sunday mornings tippling instead of praying were even
worse:

> O tell us Sir Andrew, whose puritan zeal
> To Sabbath profaners destruction shall deal,
> Did you ever behold such a sample of sin
> As church time turn-out from a Temple of Gin?
> Costermongers, coal heavers, dustmen and drabs,

Swell omnibus jarveys and drivers of cabs,
The bell chimes to church and out stagger the queer 'uns,
From Wellers in Old Street and Thompsons and Fearons.
—from *Life in London*, I.R. and
G. Cruickshank, 1822

⊰ ⊱

At 11 a.m., 18 June 1815, the Battle of Waterloo begins with a French artillery bombardment on the Chateau of Hougoumont, positioned to the extreme right of the British and allied line. The first infantry assault goes in at Hougoumont at midday (and see below, 9 p.m.).

ARMISTICE, NOVEMBER 1918

As every schoolchild knows, the First World War finally ended at the eleventh hour on the eleventh day of the eleventh month. As one military historian summed up, the response among the troops was muted – 'no cheering and very little outward excitement'. It is little wonder that the mood was, for the most part, sombre. Combat had lasted right up to the final moment, and in some cases, for some time afterwards. One unfortunate British officer, commanding a battery of six-inch howitzers, was killed by a violation of the ceasefire at one minute past eleven. At this point, his second-in-command ordered the battery to continue firing for another hour against the German lines, which did not retaliate. Elsewhere, at the Belgian village of Erquelinnes, a British captain commanding a cavalry squadron recorded that:

At 11.15 it was found necessary to end the days of a Hun machine-gunner on our front who would keep on shooting. The armistice was already in force, but there was no alternative. Perhaps his watch was wrong but he was probably the last German killed in the war – a most unlucky individual!

Sometimes the end of hostilities was marked with curious little acts of ceremony, and at times of strange humour. Near Mons, a German machine-gunner fired off his very last belt of ammunition in the last sixty seconds of hostilities, then, at 11 a.m. exactly, ceased firing, stepped up on the parapet, removed his steel helmet and bowed to his now-former enemies. Then he wandered off, presumably home.

When news of the German surrender reached him, a young German soldier, recuperating from temporary blindness in the army hospital at Pasewalk, in Pomerania, went mad with rage and grief:

> I could stand it no longer. It became impossible for me to sit still one moment more. Again everything went black before my eyes; I tottered and groped my way back to the dormitory, threw myself on my bunk, and dug my burning head into my blanket and pillow.
>
> Since the day when I had stood at my mother's grave, I had not wept... But now I could not help it...
>
> And so it had all been in vain...
>
> —Adolf Hitler, *Mein Kampf*, written c.1925-6

-◁ ▷-

MID-MORNING REFRESHMENTS

Though the habit of taking a small snack some time between breakfast and lunch is still very much with us, the name by which it used to be known – 'elevenses' – now sounds rather quaint; and the notion that it might include a reviving tot of alcohol now seems rather decadent, if appealing. A long-established London publishing house used to follow the charming tradition of supplying its employees with an elevenses consisting of a glass of Madeira and a Bath Oliver. According to his biographer, Patrick Marnham, Georges Simenon – a sickly child – was for many years given an 'elevenses' of *laits de poule a la bière* – raw eggs and sugar whipped up in (Belgian) beer. The traditional recipe calls for milk, but the future creator of Maigret had developed an allergy to milk while still a baby.

For most of us, the appropriate refreshment at this hour is a cup of coffee or tea. In Britain, the mid-morning tea-break owes its origins to an experiment proposed by the Minister of Labour in 1940, during the early months of the war. The workers of a large firm were to be allowed two mid-shift breaks for tea, one in the morning and one in the afternoon. After a month, the Minister asked the firm's directors if they would like to give up the experiment. 'Not on your life,' was the response. 'We have made too much out of it in increased productivity.'

Brunch, the American invention that, as its name suggests, cross-breeds breakfast with lunch, is generally served from about 11 a.m. onwards, particularly on Sundays or other days of leisure. In America, the food is often washed down with Bloody Marys or Mimosas (which the British know as Buck's Fizz – champagne or some other sparkling white wine and orange juice), which are particularly soothing to those brunchers who drank too freely the night before. Lord Byron's favour-ite pick-me-up for these circumstances was hock and soda:

> ... Get very drunk, and when
> You wake with headache, you shall see what then.
>
> Ring for your valet, bid him quickly bring
> Some hock and soda water. Then you'll know
> A pleasure worthy Xerxes, the great king;
> For not the blest sherbet, sublimed with snow,
> Nor the first sparkle of the desert spring,
> Nor Burgundy in all its sunset glow,
> After long travel, ennui, love or slaughter,
> Vie with that draught of hock and soda water.
> —*Don Juan*, Canto II

Eleven of the clock

It is now the eleventh hour, children must break up school, lawyers must make home to their houses, merchants to the exchange, and gallants to the ordinary; the dishes set ready for

the meat, and the glasses half full of fair water: now the market people make towards their horses, and the beggars begin to draw near the towns; the porridge, put off the fire, is set a cooling for the plough folk, and the great loaf and the cheese are set ready on the table: colleges and halls ring to dinner, and a scholar's commons is soon digested: the rich men's guests are at curtsy, and 'I thank you': and the poor man's feast is 'Welcome, and God be with you': the page is ready with his knife and his trencher, and the meat will be half cold, ere the guests can agree on their places: the cook voids the kitchen, and the butler the buttery, and the serving-men stand all ready at the dresser: the children are called to say grace before dinner, and the nice people rather look than eat: the gates be locked for fear of the beggars, and the minstrels called in to be ready with their music: the plesant wit is now breaking a jest, and the hungry man puts his jaws to their proof. In sum, to conclude my opinion of it, I hold it the epicure's joy and the labourer's ease. Farewell.

—Nicholas Breton, *The Fantasticks*, 1626

Sala on Upper-Class Weddings

Eleven o'clock in the morning. Here we are at a fashionable wedding at St James's Church, Piccadilly.

If I had the tongue or pen of 'Mr Penguin', the urbane and aristocratic correspondent of the 'Morning Post', I should give you quite a vivid, and at the same time a refined, description of that edifying spectacle – a marriage in high life. How eloquent, and, by turns, pathetic and humorous I could be on the bevy of youthful bridesmaids – all in white tulle over pink glacé silk, all in bonnets trimmed with white roses, and with bouquets of camellias and lilies of the valley! How I could expatiate, likewise, on the appearance of the beauteous and high-born bride, her Honiton lace veil, her innumerable flounces; and her noble parents, and the gallant and distinguished bridegroom, in fawn-coloured inexpressibles and a cream-coloured face; and his 'best man,' the burly colonel of the Fazimanagghur Irregulars; and the crowd of distinguished personages who alight from their carriages at the little wicket in Piccadilly, and pass along the great area amid the cheers of the little boys! They are all so noble and distinguished, that one clergyman can't perform the ceremony, and extra parsons are provided like extra oil-lamps on a gala night at Cremorne. The register becomes an autograph-book of noble and illustrious signatures; the vestry-room has sweet odours of Jockey Club and Frangipani lingering about it for hours afterwards; the pew-opener picks up white linen favours tied with silver twist. A white rose, broken short off at the stem, lies unregarded on the altar-steps; and just within the rails are some orange-blossoms from the bride's coronal. For they fall and die, the blossoms, as well as the brown October leaves. Spring has its death as well as autumn: a death followed often by no summer, but by cold and cruel winter. The blossoms fall and die, and the paths by the hawthorn hedges are strewn with their bright corses. The blossoms droop and die: the little children die, and the green velvet of the cemetery is dotted with tiny grave-stones.

See, the bridal procession comes into garish Piccadilly, and, amid fresh cheers and the pealing of joy-bells, steps into its carriages.

> 'Happy, happy, happy pair!
> None but the brave,
> None but the brave,
> None but the brave deserve the fair.'

So sings Mr John Dryden, whilom poet laureate. Let us hope that the brides of St James's are all as fair as the bridegrooms are brave, and that they all commence a career of happiness by that momentous plunge into the waters of matrimony at eleven o'clock in the morning.

—George Augustus Sala, *Twice Round the Clock*, 1858-9

EPITHALAMION

Spenser's poem, often considered the greatest verse celebration of marriage in the English language, is carefully divided into twenty-four stanzas – alluding to, rather than depicting, each hour of the day, for (unlike the present work) there is no direct correspondence between the number of the division and the hour of the clock. Here is the thirteenth stanza, celebrating the marriage service itself:

> Behold whiles she before the altar stands
> Hearing the holy priest that to her speakes
> And blesseth her with his two happy hands,
> How the red roses flush up in her cheekes,
> And the pure snow with goodly vermill stayne,
> Like crimsin dyde in grayne,
> That even th'Angels which continually,
> About the sacred Altare doe remaine,
> Forget their service and about her fly,
> Ofte peeping in her face that seems more fayre,
> The more they on it stare.
> But her sad eyes still fastened on the ground,
> Are governed with goodly modesty,
> That suffers not one looke to glaunce awry,
> Which may let in a little thought unsownd.
> Why blush ye love to give to me your hand,
> The pledge of all our band?
> Sing ye sweet Angels, Alleluya sing,
> That all the woods may answere and your eccho ring…

(Entered in the Stationer's Register in 1594 and published in 1595. It is widely believed that the poem celebrates Spenser's second marriage, to Elizabeth Boyle. According to one numerological reading, the fact that Night falls at exactly line 300 is a sign that sixteen and a quarter hours of daylight have passed since dawn – precisely the hours of daylight specified for Spenser's wedding day, 11 June 1594 – St

Barnabus's Day, in contemporary almanacs. In the Elizabethan calendar, St Barnabus's day was the date of the summer solstice, as noted in the proverb 'Barnaby bright, Barnaby bright, the longest day and the shortest night.')

⇥ ⇤

Part Two: Noon to 5 p.m.

Noon to 1 p.m.

GREENWICH MEAN TIME

Whole books have been devoted to this subject, but here are a couple of salient details for beginners.

1. Why 'Mean'?

Because the rotation of the earth is not as precise as we would find convenient in an ideal cosmos. When measured against certain celestial markers – the so-called 'fixed' or 'clock' stars – it is found to wobble slightly; the charming technical name for this wobble is nutation. (It was discovered by the third Astronomer Royal, James Bradley, who held office from 1742 to 1762.) Nor does the earth's annual journey round the sun proceed at an entirely uniform speed: as a result, 'solar' time, the time shown by sundials, can vary by as much as fifteen minutes from the more exact 'sidereal' time, the time set by observation of the stars. (The sun, you will recall, is very close to us in the grander scheme of things; the stars are, at the very least, 200,000 times farther away.)

So – sidereal time is regular, or as regular as we need it to be for most purposes; solar time varies somewhat. We say that a 'year' is exactly 365 days, but the actual solar year is more like 365 days, 5 hours, 48 minutes and 48 seconds. We fudge this difference of almost six hours by adding an extra day to our calendar every fourth year. Similarly, the average solar day of twenty-four hours is actually a little longer than the sidereal day, which is reckoned as 23 hours, 56 minutes, 4.09 seconds. So for most practical purposes, the universally agreed duration of an hour is the average – the 'mean' – of the solar day. This is Mean Time, or Greenwich Mean Time, or GMT.

2. Why Greenwich?

Because Greenwich, on the south bank of the Thames, has, since its foundation in 1675, been home to the Royal Observatory. (The stimulus for this development was, as most readers will have become well aware in the last decade or so, the urgent hunt by maritime powers for a reliable means to determine latitude at sea.) Sir Christopher Wren was the architect, and the Reverend John Flamsteed the first Astronomer Royal. From 1769 onwards, all British ships have carried Greenwich time with them, and it has been the duty of the Observatory to verify that all the chronometers issued and used by the Admiralty should give accurate time (more exactly, that their inevitable errors should be predictable to a high degree of accuracy).

In recognition of the outstanding contribution of the Observatory to nautical affairs and astronomy alike, the nations of the earth agreed to accept the meridian that runs through the Observatory as the zero or prime meridian.

The full story, needless to say, is a good deal more complex.

At noon on November 18, 1883, standard time was imposed on the United States. American cities, towns, and villages abandoned approximately forty-nine local or sun-regulated times in favor of four scientific, clock-defined zones. This new time was regulated not only by Greenwich mean time but by the Gilded Age marriage between money-grubbing telegraph companies and scientific, astronomical observatories. The telegraph, not the sun, now communicated time to a temporally unified nation and, in the process, helped pave the way for the globalization of abstracted, decontextualized world time.

— Mark M. Smith, *Mastered by the Clock: Time, Slavery and Freedom in the American South*, 1997

-╡ ╞-

LATE RISING

And sleepless Lovers, just at Twelve, awake ...
— Alexander Pope, 'The Rape of the Lock', 1712

Sunday, 26 September

I awaked at noon, with a severe head-ache. I was much vexed that I should have been guilty of such a riot, and afraid of a reproof from Dr Johnson. I though it very inconsistent with that conduct which I ought to maintain, while the companion of the Rambler. About one he came into my room, and accosted me, 'What, drunk yet?' — His tone of voice was not that of severe upbraiding; so I was relieved a little, — 'Sir, (said I,) they kept me up.' — He answered, 'No, you kept them up, you drunken dog:' — This he said with a good-humoured English pleasantry. Soon afterwards, Corrichatachin, Col, and other friends assembled round my bed. Corri had a brandy-bottle and glass with him, and insisted I should take a dram. — 'Ay, (said Dr Johnson,) fill him drunk again. Do it in the morning, that we may laugh at him all day. It is a poor thing for a fellow to get drunk at night, and sculk to bed, and let his friends have no sport.' Finding him thus jocular, I became quite easy; and when I offered to get up, he very good-naturedly said, 'You need be in no such hurry now.' — I took my host's advice, and drank some brandy, which I found an effectual cure for my head-ache. When I rose, I went into Dr Johnson's room, and taking up Mrs M'Kinnon's Prayer book, I opened it at the twentieth Sunday after Trinity, in the epistle for which I read, 'And be not drunk with wine, wherein there is excess.' Some would have taken this as a divine interposition.

—James Boswell, *A Tour of the Western Isles and Hebrides*,1785

-ᘓ ᗷ-

REDNESSE AT NOONE

About noone time wee saw *a certaine rednesse in the skie*, as a shew or messenger of the Sunne that began to come towards us... [and we] comforted each other, giving God thankes that the hardest time of Winter was past, *being in good hope that we should live to talk of those things at home in our own Countrey*.

> —The testimony of Gerrit de Veer, describing a naval journey into Arctic regions under the command of William Barrents, begun in 1596; cited in *Purchas his Pilgrimages*, Book XIII, 1625 edition

(As Livingstone Lowes demonstrated in his classic study *The Road to Xanadu*, this is one of the passages that inspired Coleridge when he was writing *The Ancient Mariner*.)

Twelve of the clock

It is now the twelfth hour, the sun is at his height, and the middle of the day: the first course is served in, and the second ready to follow: the dishes have been read over, and the reversion set by: the wine begins to be called for, and who waits not is chidden: talk passeth away time, and when stomachs are full discourses grow dull and heavy, but after fruit and cheese say grace and take away: now the markets are done, the exchange broke up, and the lawyers at dinner, and Duke Humphrey's servants make their walks in Paul's: the shopmen keep their shops, and their servants go to dinner: the traveller begins to call for a reckoning, and goes into the stable to see his horse eat his provender: the ploughman now is at the bottom of his dish, and the labourer draws out his dinner out of his bag: the beasts

of the field take rest after their feed, and the birds of the air are at juke in the bushes: the lamb lies sucking while the ewe chews the cud, and the rabbit wil scarce peep out of her burrow: the hare sits close asleep in her muse, while the dogs sit waiting for a bone from the trencher. In brief, for all I find of it, I thus conclude in it: I hold it the stomach's pleasure and the spirit's weariness. Farewell.

—Nicholas Breton, *The Fantasticks*, 1626

[reversion: the left-overs; Duke Humphrey's servants: to 'dine with Duke Humphrey' was to go without dinner – it was the habit of impoverished young men of fashion to loiter near Duke Humphey's monument in St Paul's Walk; at juke: chirping and clucking to each other]

In ancient Rome, a timekeeper would shout out the hour as the sun passed between the Rostrum and the Grecostasis. In modern Rome, a cannon is fired.

Noonday Demons were the merciless torturers of the Desert Fathers – hermits of the early Christian church. Their foul existence was hinted at in Psalm 91, verses 5– 6:

5. Thou shalt not be afraid for the terror by night; nor for the arrow that flieth by day;

6. Nor for the pestilence that walketh in darkness; nor for the destruction that wasteth at noonday.

THE NOON BALL

Until the twentieth century, most major harbours in the western world would display a huge time ball, which would fall every day at noon to give navigators a precise visual signal by which to regulate their chronometers. Vestiges of the practice survive at Greenwich, though –

where it began in 1838, though the time for the drop was set at 1 p.m., since at noon the astronomers would all be busy studying the exact position of the sun – and in the famous Times Square Ball, which falls as the chimes strike in the New Year: a sight familiar to countless millions of television viewers.

A Lecture Upon the Shadow

Stand still, and I will read to thee
A lecture, love, in love's philosophy.
These three hours that we have spent
In walking here, two shadows went
Along with us, which we ourselves produc'd.
But, now the Sun is just above our head,
We do these shadows tread;
And to brave clearness all things are reduc'd.
So, whilst our infant love did grow,
Disguises did, and shadows, flow
From us, and our cares; but now 'tis not so.

That love hath not attained the high'st degree,
Which is still diligent lest others see.

Except our love at this noon stay,
We shall new shadows make the other way.
As the first were made to blind
Others, these which come behind
Will work upon ourselves, and blind our eyes.
If once love faint, and westwardly decline,
To me thou, falsely, thine,
And I to thee mine actions shall disguise.
The morning shadows wear away,
But these grow longer all the day, –
But oh, love's day is short, if love decay.

Love is a growing, or full constant light;
And his first minute, after noon, is night.
                                        —John Donne (1572– 1631)

1 p.m. to 2 p.m.

Since 1861, the cannon at Edinburgh Castle has been fired
every day at exactly 1300 hrs.

EVEN LATER RISING

It was long past noon when he awoke. His valet had crept several
times on tiptoe into the room to see if he was stirring, and had
wondered what made his young master sleep so late. Finally his
bell sounded, and Victor came softly in with a cup of tea, and a
pile of letters, on a small tray of old Sèvres china, and drew back
the olive-satin curtains, with their shimmering blue lining, that
hung in front of the three tall windows.

'Monsieur has slept well this morning,' he said, smiling.

'What o'clock is it, Victor?' asked Dorian Gray, drowsily.

'One hour and a quarter, Monsieur.'

How late it was! He sat up, and having sipped some tea, turned
over his letters. One of them was from Lord Henry, and had been
brought by hand that morning. He hesitated for a moment, and
then put it aside. The others he opened listlessly. They contained
the usual collection of cards, invitations to dinner, tickets for
private views, programmes of charity concerts, and the like, that
are showered on fashionable young men every morning during
the season. There was a rather heavy bill for a chased silver
Louis-Quinze toilet-set, that he had not yet had the courage to
send on to his guardians, who were extremely old-fashioned

people and did not realize that we live in an age when unnecessary things are our only necessities; and there were several very courteously worded communications from Jermyn Street money-lenders offering to advance any sum of money at a moment's notice and at the most reasonable rates of interest.

After about ten minutes he got up, and, throwing on an elaborate dressing-gown of silk-embroidered cashmere wool, passed into the onyx-paved bathroom. The cool water refreshed him after his long sleep. He seemed to have forgotten all that he had gone through. A dim sense of having taken part in some strange tragedy came to him once or twice, but there was the unreality of a dream about it.

As soon as he was dressed, he went into the library and sat down to a light French breakfast, that had been laid out for him on a small round table close to the open window. It was an exquisite day. The warm air seemed laden with spices. A bee flew in, and buzzed round the blue-dragon bowl that, filled with sulphur-yellow roses, stood before him. He felt perfectly happy.

—Oscar Wilde, *The Picture of Dorian Gray*, 1891

Nineteen Eighty-Four

'It was a bright cold day in April, and the clocks were striking thirteen …': the opening line of Orwell's novel, as Anthony Burgess pointed out in his own book *1985*, is deliberately jarring to a British ear, and all the more so when Orwell's novel was new and the United Kingdom staunchly excluded continental measurements. The standard Italian translation misses the chill: '*Era una bella e fredda mattina d'Aprile e gli orologi batterono l'una*' – that is, 'one'.

Incidentally, clocks that struck all twenty-four hours were familiar in Italy from the fourteenth century onwards.

-ᴈ ᴇ-

ON LUNCH

Lunch, as we more or less know it today, came into being some time around the first decade or so of the nineteenth century, though the word and its near relatives had been around for a good deal longer. The words *nuncheon* and *nunch* can be found as early as the fourteenth century, though they seem to have slipped from popular use from about 1650 to 1750. Johnson's *Dictionary* (1755) defines 'nunchin' as 'a piece of victuals eaten between meals', and 'luncheon' or 'lunch' as 'as much food as one's hand can hold' — not a bad definition for what we might call a 'snack'. Jane Austen spelled the older word as 'noonshine' (a misfired guess at its roots?) in a letter of 1808, but three years later, in *Sense and Sensibility*, uses 'nuncheon' as the term for a hasty meal bolted down by a horseman while waiting for his mount to be rubbed down. In the following year, 1812, Maria Edgeworth uses 'lunch' both as noun and as verb in *The Absentee*:

> ... they just drove out here to see the points of view for fashion's sake ... and up with their glasses, like their ladies; and then out with their watches, and 'Isn't it time to lunch?' So there they have been lunching within on what they brought with them; for nothing in our house would they touch of course! They brought themselves a pick-nick lunch, with Madeira and Champagne to wash it down. Why, gentlemen, what do you think, but a set of them, as they were bragging to me, turned out of a boarding-house at Cheltenham, last year, because they had no peach pies to their lunch!

In *Pride and Prejudice* (1813), Elizabeth and Jane Bennet, returning from London, are given 'the nicest cold luncheon in the world'.

What was happening? Men were breakfasting a little earlier, and everyone was dining a little later. As the day grew longer, a more substantial meal at about midday became essential; or, to put it another way, it gradually dawned – especially on men of affairs – that by dining at 6 p.m., 7 p.m., or even later, the useful period of the day could be drawn out to eight or nine hours, with just a small interruption for, say, a glass of port and a biscuit. Their wives also learned the attractions of spending a good, uninterrupted stretch of the day without the nuisance of their husbands. (It can hardly be a coincidence that divorce rates began to rocket.)

By the 1830s, as we can gather from various gossipy sources, it had become the habit of ladies of leisure to consume a sizeable meal rather later in the day, around mid-afternoon. 'Women ... are not quite so irrational as men, in London, for they generally sit down to a substantial lunch about three or four; and if men would do the same, the meal at eight would be relieved of many of its weighty dishes.' Since men did not, on the whole, do the same, they would often return from the office both weary and ravenous, barely having touched food since early morning. Masculine resistance to this feminine innovation lasted a very long time, especially among those who were set in their older ways. It was not until 1853 that Macaulay – in poor health – gave in to 'the detested necessity of breaking the labours of the day by luncheon'. The principal exceptions to this male counter-revolution were to be found in the City, where the likes of Ralph Nickleby soon saw that business could be advanced by trading while eating. The business lunch has its origins here.

Still, some women also begrudged the practice of hearty midday eating. In 1853, readers of *The Family Friend* were instructed that lunch

is admissible only when either the interval between the breakfast and dinner is very prolonged, or when the quantity of food taken at breakfast is very small. The lower classes, as well as the children of the higher classes, dine early, and thus with them luncheon is unnecessary and accordingly not taken. Not so, however, with adults of the middling and higher classes; with them, either from business or other causes, the practice of dining late has become general, and, with such, luncheon becomes a necessary meal. It should be taken about five hours after breakfast, and though called by another name it may be considered a light dinner, taken to allay the cravings of nature, but not entirely to destroy the appetite.

It is striking that Mrs Beeton offers only very sketchy instruction on the matter:

> [Lunch] should be a light meal but its solidity must of course in some degree be proportionate to the time it is intended to enable you to wait for your dinner and the amount of exercise you take in the meantime ... In many houses where a nursery dinner is provided for the children about one o'clock the mistress and the elder portion of the family make their luncheon at the same time and from the same joint, or whatever may be provided ... The more usual plan is for the lady of the house to have the joint brought to her table and afterwards carried to the nursery.
>
> —*Household Management*, 1869

A major class distinction is born at about this time – a distinction that survives to the present day in many parts of Britain. The upper and managerial classes sit down to a midday lunch; workers, schoolchildren and other sitters below the salt expect to have their dinner at this hour. Now in large measure a verbal distinction, it began as a real difference in eating habits. In Mrs Henry Wood's *Roland Yorke* we meet a solicitor who, at one every day, goes upstairs from his office and joins his family for a light meal – luncheon. His clerks, meanwhile go out to eat dinner – the most substantial meal of the day. The most interesting case is that of the class intermediary, the Managing Clerk, who also goes out to eat at one, and may well eat exactly what the other clerks are eating; but he calls his meal *luncheon* to maintain the polite fiction that he, like his employer, expects to dine that evening.

Not that the officer classes were inclined to stint themselves at the midday table. Nathaniel Hawthorne (1804– 64), now remembered for his remarkable novels, was the American consul at Liverpool from 1853 to 1858. On 6 March 1856, he noted in his diary:

Yesterday I lunched on board Captain Russell's ship the *Princeton*. These daily lunches on shipboard might answer very well the purposes of a dinner; being, in fact, noonday dinners, with soup, roast mutton, mutton chops, and a macaroni pudding – brandy, port and sherry wines. There were three elderly Englishmen at table, with white heads, – which, I think, is oftener the predicament of elderly heads here than in America. One of these was a retired Customs-House officer, and the other two were connected with the shipping in some way. There is a satisfaction in seeing Englishmen eat and drink, they do it so heartily, and, on the whole, so wisely, – trusting so entirely that there is no harm in good beef and mutton, and a reasonable quantity of good liquor; and these three hale old men, who had acted on this wholesome faith so long, were proofs that it is well on earth to eat like earthly creatures. In America, what squeamishness, what delicacy, what stomachic apprehension, would there not be among three stomachs of sixty or seventy years' experience! I think this failure of American stomachs is partly due to our ill-usage of our digestive powers, and partly to our want of faith in them.

—*The English Note-Books of Nathaniel Hawthorne*, 1870

Outside the armed forces, the idea that lunch might be an agreeable social occasion as well as a chance to refuel a flagging metabolism was slow to dawn, and for many decades the lunch party was an almost entirely feminine occasion. Most of the colleges of Oxford and Cambridge served only 'commons' at lunch time: frugal servings of bread, cheese, cold meat and college ale, bought from the Buttery and eaten by the undergraduates in their rooms. This monkish convention was broken in the late 1880s by, among others, Oscar Browning, a fellow of King's College, Cambridge, who introduced an informal, talkative communal lunch with hot dishes – soup, fish, mince, rice pudding and the like. Browning wrote to a colleague at Oxford (12 May 1891):

Our common luncheon in Hall is a great success. Things are ordered a la carte. The usual prices are Soup 6d, Fish or Entree 6d, made dish 8d, cold meat 3d or 4d, Vegetables or salad 1d, Pudding 3d. Men order whatever they like but the whole style is simple. There is also a charge of 3d for bread and waiting which is imposed on Fellows as well as Undergraduates and is charged to the Buttery account.

Members of College entertain out [-of-] College friends at luncheon. The luncheon is served at the tables used for dinner and the most delightful part of the arrangement is that Dons, Undergraduates & their friends all sit together and the conversation is quite general and I may say unrestrained ...

It was the Second World War that taught the British – strictly rationed as to how much they could buy in food shops – to eat as heartily as possible outside the home at lunchtime, whether in work or forces canteens or in cheap restaurants or eating clubs. This habit persisted for many years after the war.

2 p.m. to 3 p.m.

Oscar is Humilated

Everything about my tragedy has been hideous, mean, repellent, lacking in style; our very dress makes us grotesque. We are the zanies of sorrow. We are clowns whose hearts are broken. We are specially designed to appeal to the sense of humour. On November 13th, 1895, I was brought down here from London. From two o'clock to half-past two on that day I had to stand on the centre platform of Clapham Junction in convict dress, and handcuffed, for the world to look at. I had been taken out of the hospital ward without a moment's notice being given to me. Of all possible objects I was the most grotesque. When people saw me they laughed. Each train as it came up swelled the audience. Nothing could exceed their amusement. That was, of course, before they knew who I was. As soon as they had been informed they laughed still more. For half an hour I stood there in the grey November rain surrounded by a jeering mob.

For a year after that was done to me I wept every day at the same hour and for the same space of time. That is not such a tragic thing as possibly it sounds to you. To those who are in prison tears are a part of every day's experience. A day in prison on which one does not weep is a day on which one's heart is hard, not a day on which one's heart is happy.

—Oscar Wilde, *De Profundis*

(*De Profundis* was not published in any form until a heavily expurgated version of its 50,000-word text appeared in 1905; the full version was not published until 1962.)

⊰ ⊱

ON SHOPPING

Shopping and dealing:

Behold Regent Street at two p.m. ...

Not without reason do I declare it the most fashionable street in the world. I call it not so for the aristocratic mansions it might possess; for the lower parts of the houses are occupied as shops, and the furnished apartments are let, either to music or operatic celebrities or to unostentatious old bachelors. But the shops themselves are innately fashionable. There was a dash of utilitarianism mingled with the slightly Bohemian tinge of my Regent Street of twenty years ago; there were baker's shops, stationers, and opticians, who had models of steam engines in their windows. There was a grocer not above selling orange marmalade, brown sugar, and Durham mustard. I remember buying a penny cake of chocolate of him one morning; but I find the shop now expanded into a magnificent emporium, where are sold wines, and spirits, sweetmeats and preserves, liqueurs and condiments, Bayonne ham, Narbonne honey, Bologna sausages, Russian caviare, Iceland moss, clotted cream, and *terrines* of *pâté de fois gras*. Indeed, Regent Street is an avenue of superfluities − a great trunk-road in Vanity Fair. Fancy watchmakers, haberdashers, and photographers; fancy stationers, fancy hosiers, and fancy staymakers; music shops, shawl shops, jewellers, French glove shops, perfumery, and point lace shops, confectioners and milliners: creamily, these are the merchants whose wares are exhibited in this Bezesteen of the world.

Now, whatever can her ladyship, who has been shopping in Regent Street, have ordered the stalwart footman, who shut the carriage door with a resounding bang, to instruct the coachman to drive her to the bank for? Her ladyship's own private bank is in a shiningly aristocratic street, by Cavendish Square, embosomed among green trees. She does not want to buy ribbons or lace on Ludgate Hill, artificial flowers in St Paul's Churchyard, or fine linen in Cheapside. No; she has a very simple reason for going into the city: Sir John, her liege lord, is on 'Change. He will be there from half-past two to three, at which hour High 'Change, as it may be called, closes, and she intends to call for him, and drive him to the West-end again. By your leave, we will jump up behind the carriage, heedless of the stalwart footman; for we are in the receipt of fern-seed, and invisible.

Going on 'Change seems to be but a mechanical and mercantile occupation, and one that might with safety be entrusted to some confidential clerk; yet it is not so; and the greatest magnates of commerce and finance, the Rothschilds, the Barings, the Huths, the legions of London's merchant-princes, are to be found chaffering in the quadrangle every day. In the old Exchange, they used to point out the particular column against which the elder Rothschild was wont to lean. They called the old man, too – marvellous diplomatist in financial combinations as he was – the Pillar of the Exchange. You know that the colonnades – whose ceilings are painted in such elaborate encaustic, and with such a signal result in ruin from damp and smoke – are divided into different promenades, variously designated, according to the nations of the merchants who frequent them. Thus – there are the Italian Walk, the Spanish walk, the Portuguese walk, the Danish walk, and – a very notable walk it is, too – the Greek Walk. Here you may see, jabbering and gesticulating, the crafty, keen-eyed, sallow-faced Smyrnians, Suliotes, Zantrites, and Fanariotes, individuals much given to speculations in corn, in which, if report does them no injustice, they gamble most egregiously.

Three o'clock strikes – or rather chimes – from the bell-tower of Mr Tite's new building. The quadrangle of the Exchange is converted into an accurate model of the Tower of Babel. The mass of black-hatted heads – with here and there a white one, like a fleck of foam on the crest of a wave – eddies with violence to and fro. Men shout, and push, and struggle, and jostle, and shriek bargains into one another's ears. A stranger might imagine that these money and merchandise dealers had fallen out, and were about to fight; but the beadle of the Exchange looks on calmly; he knows that no breach of the peace will be committed, and that the merchants and financiers are merely singing their ordinary paean of praise to the great god Mammon. Surely – if there be not high treason in the thought – they ought to pull down Mr Lough's statue of Queen Victoria, which stands in the centre of the quadrangle, and replace it by a neat effigy of the Golden Calf.

—George Augustus Sala, *Twice Round the Clock*, 1858– 9

But the spectacle can be a cruel experience for those without the means to do more than gaze. Here is Dreiser's Carrie in one of Chicago's new department stores, the Fair:

Carrie passed along the busy aisles, much affected by the remark-able displays of trinkets, dress goods, shoes, stationery, jewelry. Each separate counter was a show place of dazzling interest and attraction. She could not help feeling the claim of each trinket and valuable upon her personally and yet she did not stop. There was nothing there which she could not have used – nothing which she did not long to own. The dainty slippers and stockings, the delicately frilled skirts and petticoats, the laces, ribbons, hair-combs, purses, all touched her with individual desire, and she felt keenly the fact that not any of these things were in the range of her purchase. She was a work-seeker, an outcast without em-ployment, one whom the average employer could tell at a glance was poor and in need of a situation.

—*Sister Carrie*, III

※ ※

We dine at 2 and have tea with potted meat at 6.30, and no soda, no brandy, no wine save Marsala, not even thick cream, as milk is scarce; but we have health and no stuffiness, stodginess or formulae. We don't talk about the weather much.

—William Cory, 31 December 1877

As the poet and critic John Berryman once noted, the action of Shake-speare's *The Tempest* appears to begin at about two o'clock in the afternoon and lasts to about six. This means that it is one of the only two plays in the Shakespearean canon (the other is the *Comedy of Errors*) to take place in a reasonably close approximation to real time, since the standard hour for the start of a theatrical performance throughout most of Shakespeare's career was 2 p.m.

᠅

ON THE BROTHELS OF PARIS

In his charming memoir cum history *We'll Always Have Paris*, the Australian writer John Baxter notes that, in their glory days from about the 1890s until the Second World War, 2 p.m. was the traditional opening hour for the grand Parisian brothels; they would usually stay open until 2 a.m., at which time the working girls would be picked up and taken home by their 'mecs' – their pimps. The most famous houses were well known to the whole city: Le Chabanais at 12 rue Chabanais; Le Sphinx at 31 boulevard Edgar Quinet, across the road from the Montparnasse cemetery (which today holds the mortal remains of Jean-Paul Sartre and Simone de Beauvoir); 6 rue des Moulins, where Toulouse-Lautrec dashed off his celebrated brothel studies; and Le One-Two-Two at 122 rue de Provence.

It is hard to overstate the significance of these houses in French public and private life. They thrived under various names – *maisons de tolerance* or tolerated houses, *maisons closes* or closed houses, and *maisons de fantasie*, houses of illusion. Only women were allowed to manage the premises, though they were invariably owned by men. The house at 12 rue Chabanais, for example, was founded by a rich and eminent member of the Jockey Club. He was wealthy and house-proud enough to have bought the entire Japanese Chamber that had won first prize at the 1896 Universal Exposition and installed it at number 12 as a permanent attraction. Edward VII was a regular; since he was unusually stout, special furniture was provided to make his erotic bouts less uncomfortable for client and lady alike.

On his first arrival in Paris, Salvador Dali immediately asked his taxi driver to take him to a brothel. The cabbie duly took him to 12 rue Chabanais, where the madame conducted him to a room supplied with multiple keyholes – one looking out into the public lounge, one looking into a bedroom. By the time he staggered out several hours later, Dali recalled, he had amassed enough erotic matter to last him a lifetime of daydreams.

The Golden Age came to an end in 1946, when a moralist and heroine of the First World War by the name of Marthe Richard launched a scheme to close down all the brothels in France. Their grand furnishings were all sold off at public auction. Of course, prostitution continued; but from now on in less opulent and – as it were – respectable guises.

> Stands the church clock at ten to three?
> And is there honey still for tea?
> —Rupert Brooke, 'The Old Vicarage,
> Grantchester', 1912

3 p.m. to 4 p.m.

An English author is struck by lighting in Turkey:

> I began to look for shelter. The silence became heavier, more insistent. The clouds were moving swiftly now, sinister and certain, gathering themselves; grey and purple, flecked with white and scarred with bronze. The hills humped and crouched. The sun went out suddenly, but still in the distance I could see the long braiding of gold on the city walls.
>
> Then the thunder spoke for the first time, like the growl of a marauding beast. The storm had cleared its throat. I felt a little afraid. I have always been afraid of thunder.
>
> The clouds were racing up behind and over me. The light deepened perceptibly to a sulphurous green, light going down steadily, dimming. The land changed. The proximity of the storm grew unbearable. It was all about and suddenly I felt in the very centre of it, very isolated and naked. It became quieter, the air and the atmosphere growing taut, delicately strung, a membrane which quivered every time the thunder grunted. And the

small world flinched, waiting for the annunciation of lightning and the roll of drums. There was no shelter and I stopped and waited, resigned to a soaking.

An abrupt chill wind shuddered the bushes and rasped through the dying, tawny grass. For a few moments all was poised, like a great mass balanced on the edge of an abyss.

Then it sprang, the thunder exploded, the lightning sweeping from its scabbard and ripping open the clouds with a crash like a splitting mountain and the roar of a falling hill. Two hundred yards away a tree was cloven as you might split a cane. A hundred yards nearer there was a detonation in the middle of the road. I seemed to be in the pupil of the storm, right in the line of a 'stick' of lightning. I shivered; stood transfixed as the sky quaked. I was sure I was the next target and there was nothing I could do. Nothing at all.

Suddenly the bicycle and I were united and we shook together. A blue light fizzed and crackled: an aureole which juggled us about for a fractional second. There was a burning smell. Then I felt as if I had been hit by a boulder. The bicycle was wrenched out of my hands.

I was lying by the side of the road when I came round in the pouring rain. My watch had stopped at precisely three o'clock. Nor could I ever make it go again. It was a timeless comment on a narrow escape. The bicycle was bent. It was the rubber handle-grips and my rubber shoes that did the trick.

—J. A. Cuddon, *The Owl's Watchsong*, 1960

-᠄ ᠄-

ON SIESTAS

Siesta – from *Sextus*, the canonical sixth hour: that is, 3 p.m. Early British travellers to the warmer countries of the South were almost invariably struck by the oddity of the practice of taking a prolonged nap during the hottest hours, and often remained stubbornly awake when it would have made far more sense to follow the local customs (hence: mad dogs and Englishman go out in the midday Sun). Some, however, saw the attraction:

There is a certain melancholy, though not displeasing influence, in the advent of a Southern summer. The long days when the heat forbids active exercise abroad, and enjoins quiet at home, following each other in bright yet monotonous succession, induce a physical languor which begets a dreamy mood. The very brilliancy of the weather, unbroken for weeks by a single change, chastens the buoyancy which the variety of other seasons awakens, and the many hours that are passed in the airy solitude of lofty apartments are rather calculated to subdue than excite. The *siesta* and the bath take the place of the opera and the promenade. Repose becomes a luxury, and thrown back upon itself the mind is prone to quiet musing and the imagination to soothing flights...

—Henry T. Tuckerman, *Isabel; or, Sicily,*
a Pilgrimage, 1839

... When he awoke, the golden sunlight of a tropical afternoon shone aslant into the court, and the atmosphere was of a still, dreamy character, that seemed to invite to indolent repose all living things. It was the voluptuous hour of the *siesta*, when the dwellers in southern climes resign themselves to the drowsy influence of the time, and households and cities are buried in the deep repose of midnight, until the evening breezes, that stir the lethargic air, awaken them with renewed life and energies.

—J.H. Ingram, *The Quadroone; or,*
St Michael's Day, 1841

'Monday at 3: such an *obscure* hour.'
—Mrs Cornish: comment on plans for French reading
(C. H. K. Marten, Eton 1939)

Paul Fussell suggests that it is vulgar to drink a Bloody Mary after 3 p.m. (The author is fond of them at almost any hour, under the right circumstances, and vulgarity be damned.)

-᚛ ᚜-

ON FOOTBALL

Historians of the game suggest that the convention of starting play at 3 p.m. on Saturday afternoons has its origins in the Factory Act of 1850, which permitted workers in some industries (mostly the manufacturing industries of the North) to quit work at 2 p.m. on that day. With the coming of floodlit stadia, international tournaments and television investment, the timing of matches is now far more fluid than it was in those simpler days; but for most British followers of the Beautiful Game, 3 p.m. is still the hour for pulses to start racing and ribald commentary to begin.

The League Goals of Alan J. Pinkney and Other Observations

T.S. Eliot at Selhurst Park, 1971– 1997 (and possibly beyond)

i

Half past three

and we still haven't forced a corner.
The dripping Bovril our only drink.
The bloody hotdog our only food.

Do I dare
make my way up to the conveniences
at the top of the Holmesdale?

Midwinter spring is its own season,

end-to-end stuff yet goalless at half time.
I sometimes wonder if that is what Big Mal meant –
among other things – when he said that football
was a game of four halves.

la la la

ii
Oh Lord

there is no end of it, the clueless wailing
of Eagles Eagles Eagles
(to the tune of Amazing Grace)
voices singing out of empty beer cans.
I do not think that they will sing to me.

And then the raising of the scarves.

The football does not matter.
There is only the fight to recover
what has been lost
and found and lost again and again:
and now without a midfield general
like Kember to win the ball.

Twit twit twit

iii

Twenty odd years largely wasted, time before
and time after, always returning
to eighteenth position in Division Two. La la la.

April is the cruellest month, making
relegation a mathematical probability

in the last game at Highbury.

No! I'm not Kenny Sansom, nor was meant to be.

Here I am, an old misery with a dry mouth,
being stared at by away fans, waiting for a goal.
I was neither at the Spurs game,
nor half pissed on the special from Stoke, heaving
out of the window, surprised by Leeds fans,
fought. O O O O this South East Twenty Five drag –

It's so inelegant
so unintelligent.

Saaf luuunduuun la la la
saaf luuunduun la la la

God, it drives me mad.

iv

The scoreboard read
'Four o'clock'
(and flashed the attendance underneath).

In the waning dusk past half-cut features I cried
and heard another's voice cry:
'What! Are you here? Proctor, you old bugger.'

And he: 'Last season's team was relegated,
just face up to it, Pete. Shaw, Salako …
Once is enough. Pray they be
forgiven.' Alas. He left me
with a wave and a 'Cheerio'
and faded on the fulltime whistle.

'Five o'clock.'

I stopped off at The Cherry Trees
for a quick pint
(jug jug) and reflected:
'Well now that's done: and I'm glad it's over,
Glad all over, yes, yes,
I'm feeling glad all over.'

By Norwood Junction
I can connect
nothing with nothing

St James Park Anfield Crewe Alexandra
Villa Burnden Park
Get real

Ooo aah ooo aah ooo aah George Ndah

Ta ta goonight ta ta

la la la wallala leila la

DA DA DA

Notes on 'Pinkney and other Observations'

Not only the title, but the plan and a good deal of the incidental symbolism of the poem were suggested by Malcolm Allison's autobiography *Colours of my Life* (Everest 1975).

l.2 A phenomenon which I have often observed.

l. 26 Stephen David Kember was born in Croydon on December

8th, 1948, during a period of severe postwar rationing. He ended his playing days with Vancouver Whitecaps.

l. 30 I refer to what is now known as 'The Endsleigh League Division One'.

l. 34 Kenneth Graham Sansom was born in 1958; his transfer to Arsenal on August 14th, 1980 precipitated what came to be known as the 'left back' syndrome at Selhurst and a swift decline in the club's fortunes.

ll. 38– 40 cf. 'Preposterous Tales' (I Ludicrous)
('I once saw the Palace score four goals / away from home')

l. 59 The Cherry Trees still sits conveniently near to Norwood Junction; it has, to my mind, one of the finest interiors of the area's post-match watering holes. There are, to the best of my knowledge, no actual cherry trees on the premises.

l. 71 George Ndah is now, happily, back in favour with the club after a spell on loan to AFC Bournemouth.

John Stanley Procter, although a mere spectator and not indeed a 'character', is yet the most important personage in the poem, uniting all the rest. He stands for all those thousands, so many, who came along to watch a game of football and found something else there instead.

—Peter Carpenter, *Choosing an England,* 1997

⊰ ⊱

Immanuel Kant (1724– 1804), one of the greatest of all modern philosophers, was a man of strictly punctual habits. Every afternoon he would take a healthy stroll down a long avenue lined with linden trees, which thus became known as the Philosopher's Walk. So exact were his ways that his neighbours in Königsberg were able to set their clocks to 3.30 p.m. when he appeared at his front door dressed for the constitutional.

-⊰ ⊱-

4 p.m. to 5 p.m.

VICTORIAN VALUES

The Household Cavalry mounted guard is inspected every day of the year at exactly 4 p.m. According to regimental tradition – relayed to the author by Lt. Col. A. Jackson, MBE, LVO (the author's father) – the origins of this inspection are to be found in Queen Victoria's reign. One afternoon at four, the monarch was driven through the gate at Horse Guards, and the soldiers failed to recognize her. Infuriated, she declared that a full inspection be held at that hour for the next hundred years. The centenary of that idle moment has long since passed, but the practice has been maintained.

A SELECTION OF EIGHTEENTH-CENTURY DINNERS

By the eighteenth century, the hour of 'dinner' had slipped back to 4 p.m.

A relatively humble dinner for six:

> I gave them for dinner a dish of fine Tench which I had caught out of my brother's Pond in Pond Close this morning, Ham, and 3 Fowls boiled, a Plumb pudding; a couple of Ducks roasted, a roasted neck of Pork, a Plumb Tart and an Apple Tart, Pears, Apples and Nutts after dinner; White Wine and red, Beer and Cyder. Coffee and Tea in the evening at six o'clock. Hashed

Fowl and Duck and Eggs and Potatoes etc. for supper. We did
not dine until four o'clock – nor supped till ten.
                              —Parson Woodforde, 1740– 1803

La Rochefoucauld:

So the day passes till 4 o'clock, but at 4 o'clock precisely you must
present yourself in the drawing-room with a great deal more
ceremony than we are accustomed to in France. This sudden
change of social manners is quite astonishing and I was deeply
struck by it. In the morning you come down in riding boots and
a shabby coat, you sit where you like, you behave exactly as if you
were by yourself, no one takes any notice of you, and it is all
extremely comfortable. But in the evening, unless you have just
arrived, you must be well-washed and well-groomed. The standard of politeness is uncomfortably high – strangers go first into
the dining-room and sit near the hostess and are served in senior-
ity in accordance with a rigid etiquette. In fact for the first few
days I was tempted to think that it was done for a joke.

Dinner is one of the most wearisome of English experiences,
lasting, as it does, for four or five hours. The first two hours are
spent in eating... After the sweets you are given water in small
bowls of very clear glass in order to rinse out your mouth – a
custom which strikes me as extremely unfortunate. The more
fashionable folk do not rinse out their mouths but that seems to
me even worse; for, if you use the water to wash your hands, it
becomes dirty and quite disgusting. This ceremony over, the
cloth is removed... At this point all the servants disappear. The
ladies drink a glass or two of wine and at the end of half an hour
all go out together. It is then that the real enjoyment begins –
there is not an Englishman who is not supremely happy at this
particular moment... This is the time I like best; conversation is
as free as it can be, everyone expresses his political opinions with
as much frankness as he would employ upon personal subjects...
At the end of two or three hours a servant announces that tea is

ready and conducts the gentlemen from their drinking to join the ladies in the drawing-room where they are usually employed in taking tea and coffee. After taking tea, one generally plays whist, and at midnight there is cold meat for those who are hungry. While the game is going on, there is punch on the table for those who want it.

—*A Frenchman in England,* 1784

I scarcely saw my husband except at breakfast, which we ate together, and at dinner. My father-in-law had ceased to give big dinners [because of the Revolution] but we always sat down twelve or fifteen at table, what with deputies or foreigners or persons of importance. Dinner was at four. An hour after dinner, spent in the drawing-room talking to various people who had dropped in for coffee, my father-in-law went back to his office. Unless I was going on somewhere, I then returned home.

—Madame la Marquise de la Tour du Pin, *Journal d'une Femme de Quinquante Ans,* winter of 1789– 90 (she was aged nineteen)

Dinner time grows later from this point on, though not for everyone:

If you can come next Sunday we shall be equally glad to see you … Leg of Lamb, as before, hot at 4. And heart of Lamb ever.

—Charles Lamb to Thomas Allsop, 30 March 1821

-≼ ≽-

Ancient Mariner

We have been on another tour: we set out last Monday evening at half-past four. The evening was dark and cloudy; we went eight miles, William and Coleridge employing themselves in laying the plan of a ballad, to be published with some pieces of William's.

Thus Dorothy Wordsworth, writing on Monday, 20 November 1797. 'Last Monday' was therefore the 13th; so we can establish that Coleridge began work on 'The Rime of the Ancient Mariner' at 4.30 p.m. on 13 November 1797. He had completed it by the evening of 23 March 1798, when he went to dine with the Wordsworths at Alfoxden, and 'brought his ballad finished'.

OPENING HOURS IN THE COUNTRY, *c.* 1890

As it was getting on for five, we four held a consultation, and Gowing suggested that we should make for 'The Cow and Hedge' and get some tea. Stillbrook said: 'A brandy-and-soda was good enough for him.' I reminded him that all public houses were closed till six o'clock. Stillbrook said: 'That's all right – *bona fide* travellers.'

We arrived; and as I was trying to pass, the man in charge of the gate said: 'Where from?' I replied: 'Holloway.' He immediately put up his arm, and declined to let me pass. I turned back for a moment, when I saw Stillbrook, closely followed by Cummings and Gowing, make for the entrance. I watched them, and thought I would have a good laugh at their expense. I heard the porter say: 'Where from?' When, to my surprise, in fact disgust, Stillbrook replied: 'Blackheath,' and the three were immediately admitted.

Gowing called to me across the gate, and said: 'We shan't be a minute.' I waited for them the best part of an hour. When they appeared they were all in most excellent spirits, and the only one who made an effort to apologise was Mr Stillbrook, who said to me: 'It was very rough on you to be kept waiting, but we had another spin for S. and B.'s.' I walked home in silence; I couldn't speak to them. I felt very dull all the evening, but deemed it advisable *not* to say anything to Carrie about the matter.

—*The Diary of a Nobody,* George and
Weedon Grossmith, 1892

VISITING HOURS

The paying and receiving of afternoon calls among the leisured classes has always tended to be quite intricately coded, and never more so than in the world of Edith Wharton's Old New York. Ceremonial calls – paid to offer thanks for gifts, dinners, balls or other modes of entertainment – were to be expected between about three and four. Semi-ceremonial calls, usually between family members on relatively formal occasions, such the announcement of an engagement to be married, happened between four and five. Visits between close friends occurred between five and six. Ignorance of these nuances branded one as an outsider or newcomer; deliberate violation of the rules could be the occasion of scandal. Wharton occasionally makes such gaffes into important turning-points of her plots, as in *The House of Mirth*:

> Four o'clock found her in the drawing-room: she was sure that Selden would be punctual. But the hour came and passed – it moved on feverishly, measured by her impatient heart-beats. She had time to take a fresh survey of her wretchedness, and to fluctuate anew between the impulse to confide in Selden and the dread of destroying his illusions. But as the minutes passed the need of throwing herself on his comprehension became more urgent: she could not bear the weight of her misery alone. There would be a perilous moment, perhaps: but could she not trust to her beauty to bridge it over, to land her safe in the shelter of his devotion?
>
> But the hour sped on and Selden did not come. Doubtless he had been detained, or had misread her hurriedly scrawled note, taking the four for a five. The ringing of the door-bell a few minutes after five confirmed this supposition, and made Lily hastily resolved to write more legibly in future. The sound of steps in the hall, and of the butler's voice preceding them, poured fresh energy into her veins. She felt herself once more the alert and competent moulder of emergencies, and the remembrance of her power over Selden flushed her with sudden confidence.

But when the drawing-room door opened it was Rosedale who came in ...

—*The House of Mirth*, 1905

Rosedale has come, we soon discover, with an unwelcome proposal of marriage. Lily treats him rather haughtily, but he seems immune to her coolness. Both parties have broken the social contract, Rosedale because he has come at a time inappropriate to their degree of intimacy, Lily because she has neglected to tell her servants that she is not 'At Home' to anyone except Lawrence Selden.

The same set of conventions add piquancy to a well-known visiting scene in *The Age of Innocence*, in which Newland Archer pays a visit to the 'scandalous' Madame Olenska, only to find that he is not her only gentleman caller.

⊰ ⊱

A society lady, notorious for her pursuit of celebrities, once sent George Bernard Shaw an invitation reading 'Lady —— will be at home on Tuesday between four and six o'clock.' Shaw returned the card with the hand-written addition: 'Mr Bernard Shaw likewise.'

In Hogarth's painting *The Lady's Last Stake*, the clock on the mantel-piece shows 4.55 p.m. The story is not hard to make out: the Lady, a gambler, has incurred a debt that will fall due in five minutes, and if she cannot pay it off in the conventional way, she will have to find some other way of satisfying the Gentleman in the picture.

⤙ ⤚

5 p.m. to 6 p.m.

'Five o'clock Follies': the derisive term used by journalists for the daily press briefings issued by the United States military during the Vietnam War. See Michael Herr, *Despatches*.

AFTERNOON TEA TIME

The French name for afternoon or High Tea is *le five-o'clock:* hence the advertisements, baffling to uninitiated English speakers, for *le five-o'clock à toute heure*. Like the hour for dinner, if somewhat less dramatically, the hour for tea seems to have slipped back from its original hour of about 4 p.m., though not in a uniform manner. According to Lady Laura Troubridge (1926), 'the usual tea hour is 4.30'. The same authority suggests that the correct visiting hours for 'At Home' days are from 4 to 5.30 p.m. Garden Parties should run from 4 to 6.30 p.m. or 3.30 to 6.30 p.m. But in *Alice in Wonderland* (see below), the Mad Hatter's Tea Party is being held, perpetually, as late as 6 p.m.; and there is plenty of evidence to suggest that by the end of the nineteenth century five o'clock was held to be the most fashionable hour at which to take tea. Its invention has been credited to a Duchess of Bedford, though more recent historians have cast doubt on the attribution. But there can be no doubt as to the popularity of the meal, which provided a welcome pick-me-up for those who would otherwise have been forced to survive from lunchtime to 8 p.m. or later without a scrap of refreshment. The meal has inevitable connotations of England or Anglophilia, and of gentility. Anyone can wolf down a breakfast, but tea is somehow felt to be the preserve of the leisured classes, and an arena for the exercise of civility.

It finds its most elevated literary celebration as the (implausible) overture to one of the greatest novels in the English language, Henry James's *The Portrait of a Lady*:

Under certain circumstances there are few hours in life more agreeable than the hour dedicated to the ceremony of afternoon tea. There are circumstances in which, whether you partake of the tea or not – some people of course never do – the situation is in itself delightful. Those that I have in mind in beginning to unfold this simple history offered an admirable setting to an innocent pastime. The implements of the little feast had been disposed upon the lawn of an old English country house in what I should call the perfect middle of a splendid summer afternoon. Part of the afternoon had waned, but much of it was left, and what was left was of the finest and rarest quality. Real dusk would not arrive for many hours; but the flood of summer light had begun to ebb, the air had grown mellow, the shadows were long upon the smooth, dense turf. They lengthened slowly, however, and the scene expressed that sense of leisure still to come which is perhaps the chief source of one's enjoyment of such a scene at such an hour. From five o'clock to eight is on certain occasions a little eternity; but on such an occasion as this the interval could be only an eternity of pleasure. The persons concerned in it were taking their pleasure quietly, and they were not of the sex which is supposed to furnish the regular votaries of the ceremony I have mentioned. The shadows on the perfect lawn were straight and angular; they were the shadows of an old man sitting in a deep wicker-chair near the low table on which the tea had been served, and of two younger men strolling to and fro, in desultory talk, in front of him. The old man had his cup in his hand; it was an unusually large cup, of a different pattern from the rest of the set and painted in brilliant colours. He disposed of its contents with much circumspection, holding it for a long time close to his chin, with his face turned to the house. His companions had either finished their tea or were indifferent to their privilege; they smoked cigarettes as they continued to stroll. One of them, from time to time, as he passed, looked with a certain attention at the elder man, who, unconscious of observation, rested his eyes upon the rich red front of his dwelling. The house that rose beyond the lawn was a structure to repay such consideration and was the most characteristic object in the peculiarly English picture I have attempted to sketch ...

-=‡ ‡=-

THE POETS AT TEA

1. *Macaulay, who made it*

Pour, varlet, pour the water,
 The water steaming hot!
A spoonful for each man of us,
 Another for the pot!
We shall not drink from amber,
 No Capuan slave shall mix
For us the snows of Athos
 With port at thirty-six;
Whiter than snow the crystals
 Grown sweet 'neath tropic fires,
More rich the herb of China's field,
The pasture-lands more fragrance yield;
For ever let Britannia wield
 The teapot of her sires!

2. *Tennyson, who took it hot*

I think that I am drawing to an end:
For on a sudden came a gasp for breath,
And stretching of the hands, and blinded eyes,
And a great darkness falling on my soul.
O Hallelujah! ... Kindly pass the milk.

3. Swinburne, who let it get cold

As the sin that was sweet in the sinning
　　Is foul in the ending thereof,
As the heat of the summer's begining
　　Is past in the winter of love:
O purity, painful and pleading!
　　O coldness, ineffably grey!
O hear us, our handmaid unheeding,
　　And take it away!

4. Cowper, who thoroughly enjoyed it

The cosy fire is bright and gay,
The merry kettle boils away
　　And hums a cheerful song.
I sing the saucer and the cup;
Pray, Mary, fill the teapot up,
　　And do not make it strong.

5. Browning, who treated it allegorically

Tst! Bah! We take as another case –
　　Pass the pills on the window-sill; notice the capsule
(A sick man's fancy, no doubt, but I place
　　Reliance on trade-marks, Sir) – so perhaps you'll
Excuse the digression – this cup which I hold
　　Light-poised – Bah, it's spilt in the bed! – well,
　　　　let's on go –
Held Bohea and sugar, Sir; if you were told
　　The sugar was salt, would the Bohea be Congo?

6. *Wordsworth, who gave it away*

'Come, little cottage girl, you seem
   To want my cup of tea;
And will you take a little cream?
   Now tell the truth to me.'

She had a rustic, woodland grin,
   Her cheek was soft as silk,
And she replied, 'Sir, please put in
   A little drop of milk.'

'Why, what put milk into your head?
   'Tis cream my cows supply';
And five times to the child I said,
   'Why, pig-head, tell me why?'

'You call me pig-head,' she replied;
   'My proper name is Ruth.
I call that milk' – she blushed with pride –
   'You bade me speak the truth.'

7. *Poe, who got excited over it*

Here's a mellow cup of tea – golden tea!
What a world of rapturous thought its fragrance
   brings to me!
   Oh, from out the silver cells
   How it wells!
   How it smells!
Keeping tune, tune, tune, tune
To the tintinnabulation of the spoon.
And the kettle on the fire
Boils its spout off with desire,

With a desperate desire
And a crystalline endeavour
Now, now to sit, or never,
On the top of the pale-faced moon,
But he always came home to tea, tea, tea, tea, tea,
    T to the *n*-th.

8. Rossetti, who took six cups of it

The lilies lie in my lady's bower
  (O weary mother, drive the cows to roost),
They faintly droop for a little hour;
My lady's head droops like a flower.
She took the porcelain in her hand
  (O weary mother, drive the cows to roost);
She poured; I drank at her command;
Drank deep, and now – you understand!
  (O weary mother, drive the cows to roost).

9. Burns, who liked it adulterated

Weel, gin ye speir, I'm no inclined,
Whusky or tay – to state my mind
  For ane or ither;
For, gin I tak the first, I'm fou,
And gin the next, I'm dull as you,
  Mix a' thegither.

10. Walt whitman, who didn't stay more
than a minute

One cup for my self-hood,
Many for you. *Allons, camerados*, we will drink together
O hand-in-hand! That tea-spoon, please, when
  you've done with it.

What butter-colour'd hair you've got. I don't want
   to be personal.
All right, then, you needn't – you're a stale –
   cadaver.
Eighteen-pence if the bottles are returned,
Allons, from all bat-eyed formules.

                    —Barry Pain (1867– 1928)

⊰ ⊱

Frederick II (Frederick the Great, 1712– 86), King of Prussia, once noticed that one of his soldiers sported a fancy watch chain of which he was very proud, even though he was too poor to own a proper watch and had instead fastened a bullet to its free end. Deciding to have a bit of fun, Frederick pulled out his own watch – a splendid, diamond-encrusted creation – and said, 'My watch tells me that it is five o'clock. What time does yours tell?' Either quick-witted or vastly loyal, the soldier replied, 'My watch does not tell me the hour, but tells me every minute that it is my duty to die for Your Majesty.' Frederick was so delighted by the reply that he handed over his own watch, saying, 'Take this, so that you may be able to tell the hour also.'

Le Cinq a Sept: traditionally the period in which French gentlemen visit their mistresses, before returning home to their families for dinner. The phrase is so well known that the feminist film maker Agnes Varda was able to make a play on it with the title of her film *Cleo de 5 à 7,* the heroine of which is not engaging in adulterous play but anxiously awaiting the outcome of a medical examination.

Des Esseintes, the anti-hero of Huysmans's novel *A Rebours*, rises from his daylight slumbers and takes a light breakfast of boiled eggs at 5 p.m.

Five o'clock in the afternoon is also the standard waking time during the Christmas holiday season for the young UHBs (members of New

York's 'Urban Haute Bourgoisie', as one character explains the coinage) in Whit Stillman's charming film *Metropolitan* (1989).

-≒ ≓-

'Five o'clock shadow': the rather disreputable-looking stain that disfigures the jowls of men with unusually dark or dense facial hair around the end of the working day. The author recalls, as a cartoon-loving child, being mildly baffled by the lines on the faces of such characters as Fred Flintstone and Officer Dibble, clearly intended by the artists to represent the limits of their beard zones.

But also a harrowing poem by Sir John Betjeman:

Five o'Clock Shadow

This is the time of day when we in the Men's Ward
   Think 'One more surge of the pain and I give up the fight,'
When he who struggles for breath can struggle less strongly:
   This is the time of day which is worse than night.

A haze of thunder hangs on the hospital rose-beds,
   A doctor's foursome out on the links is played,
Safe in her sitting-room Sister is putting her feet up:
   This is the time of day when we feel betrayed.

Below the windows, loads of loving relations
   Rev in the car park, changing gear at the bend,
Making for home and a nice big tea and the telly:
   'Well, we've done what we can. It can't be long till the end.'

This is the time of day when the weight of bedclothes
   Is harder to bear than a sharp incision of steel.

The endless anonymous croak of a cheap transistor
   Intensifies the lonely terror I feel.
                    —From *High and Low,* 1966

-ᴈ ᴇ-

'Well, God has arrived. I met him on the 5.15 train.'
    —John Maynard Keynes to his wife Lydia, announcing
       the return to Cambridge of the great philosopher
          Ludwig Wittgenstein, 18 January 1929

According to an essay entitled 'Death and Destiny' by his modern biographer, Richard Holmes, Shelley's watch stopped at exactly sixteen minutes past five on the afternoon of 8 July 1822, when his boat, the *Don Juan,* went down under full sail in the Gulf of Spezia, about ten miles west of Viareggio. In his inspired and idiosyncratic book about the peasant-poet John Clare, *Edge of the Orison* (2005), Iain Sinclair tells the amusing story of how he baffled two Oxford librarians by apparently being able to tell by 'dowsing' which of two antique watches had been Shelley's at the time of his death. The stunt was easy: Sinclair had recently read Holmes's article, and picked the one that told the appropriate time. But Sinclair also noticed an inaccuracy: this watch actually read eighteen minutes past five. Had Holmes been inaccurate, or has the watch somehow been wound on by two minutes?

-ᴈ ᴇ-

COCKTAILS

5.30 p.m.: for much of the twentieth century, the conventional start of cocktail time. According to some sources, the world's first modern cocktail party was held in 1924, and hosted by the writer Alec Waugh, brother of the more famous novelist Evelyn. It was held at the Haverstock Hill home of the painter C. W. Nevinson. Since the idea of holding a drinks party at 5.30 p.m. seemed too outré for more conservative spirits, only one guest showed up. The next attempt was far more successful: Waugh invited thirty people 'to tea', and served them immensely strong drinks from a teapot. Everyone became riotously drunk, the evening was a great success and the cocktail era of the 1920s was launched.

The immediate forebear of Cocktail Hour was the Green Hour, *l'heure verte*, given over to the consumption of absinthe – *la fée verte*, the Green Fairy. Sources fail to agree as to whether the precise time of the Green Hour was 5, 6 or even 7 p.m., but it obviously served the same function as Cocktail Hour: to render the drinker unwilling or unable to do any more serious work, and to launch the evening's revelry. 'A glass of absinthe,' Oscar Wilde once claimed, 'is the most poetical thing in the world.' It was banned by the French authorities in 1914.

Its successor has been Happy Hour, originally an American institution: in the hope of attracting business from tired customers who could not quite face the full horrors of the rush-hour journey home, bars would offer drinks at cheap prices – often two for one – and sometimes free snacks as well. The practice proved so successful that many bars would also offer Happy Hour deals at 10 or 11 p.m., aimed at the post-dinner crowd. The most extravagant Happy Hour deal I have ever encountered was in a bar called the Plush Horse, in Huntsville, Alabama, *c.*1983. In the final days before they went out of business for good, the management were offering seventeen drinks for the price of one. Happy days.

At about the same period, I invented a cocktail that became fashionable for a few weeks or so at a bar called Close Quarters, in Nashville, Tennessee.

The Caribou

Over a fair quantity of ice, pour a large measure of Rémy Martin. Add an equal measure of Bushmill's Irish Whiskey. Bearing in mind that the brandy has already made this a fairly sweet drink, add a small measure of Kahlua to taste. Serve with two bent straws to represent Caribou antlers.

The drink, which to be perfectly honest I found mildly revolting, was devised according to a purely auditory conceit: KAH-lua; RE-my Martin; BU-shmills: KAH-RE-BU, Caribou. It seemed like a good idea at the time.

-⊰ ⊱-

It was a cold still afternoon with a hard steely sky overhead, when he [Mole] slipped out of the warm parlour into the open air. The country lay bare and entirely leafless around him, and he thought that he had never seen so far and so intimately into the insides of things as on that winter day when Nature was deep in her annual slumber and seemed to have kicked the clothes off. Copses, dells, quarries and all hidden places, which had been mysterious mines for exploration in leafy summer, now exposed themselves and their secrets pathetically, and seemed to ask him to overlook their shabby poverty for a while, till they could riot in rich masquerade as before, and trick and entice him with the old deceptions. It was pitiful in a way, and yet cheering – even exhilarating. He was glad that he liked the country undecorated, hard, and stripped of its finery. He had got down to the bare bones of it, and they were fine and strong and simple. He did not want the warm clover and the play of seeding grasses; the screens of quickset, the billowy drapery of beech and elm seemed best away; and with great cheerfulness of spirit he pushed on towards the Wild Wood, which lay before him low and threatening, like a black reef in some still southern sea.

There was nothing to alarm him at first entry. Twigs cracked under his feet, logs tripped him, funguses on stumps resembled caricatures, and startled him for the moment by their likeness to something familiar and far away; but that was all fun, and exciting. It led him on, and he penetrated to where the light was less, and trees crouched nearer and nearer, and holes made ugly mouths at him on either side.

Everything was very still now. The dusk advanced on him steadily, rapidly, gathering in behind and before; and the light seemed to be draining away like flood-water.
Then the faces began.

—Kenneth Grahame, *The Wind in the Willows*, 1908

Part Three: 6 p.m. to Midnight

6 p.m. to 7 p.m.

In his *Annals of the World* (1650), Archbishop John Ussher declared: 'The World was created on 22 October 4004 BC, at six o'clock in the evening.'

> Even is come; and from the dark Park, hark!
> The signal of the setting sun – one gun!
> And six is sounding from the chime, prime time
> To go and see the Drury-Lane Dane slain, –
> Or hear Othello's jealous doubt spout out, –
> Or Macbeth raving at that shade-made blade,
> Denying to his frantic clutch much touch; –
> Or else to see Ducrow with wide stride ride
> Four horses as no other man can span;
> Or in the small Olympic Pit, sit split
> Laughing at Liston, while you quiz his phiz ...
> —Thomas Hood, 'A Nocturnal Sketch', cited
> by W.H. Auden in *A Certain World:*
> *A Commonplace Book*, 1971

(But in subsequent decades, the theatres began to open later in the evening – see below, 7 p.m.)

Alice Discusses Time at the Mad Hatter's Tea Party

Alice sighed wearily. 'I do think you might do something better with the time,' she said, 'than wasting it in asking riddles that have no answers.'

'If you knew Time as well as I do,' said the Hatter, 'you wouldn't talk about wasting *it*. It's *him*.'

'I don't know what you mean,' said Alice.

'Of course you don't!' the Hatter said, tossing his head contemptuously. 'I dare say you never even spoke to Time!'

'Perhaps not,' Alice cautiously replied; 'but I know I have to beat time when I learn music.'

'Ah! That accounts for it,' said the Hatter. 'He wo'n't stand beating. Now, if you only kept on good terms with him, he'd do almost anything you like with the clock. For instance, suppose it were nine o'clock in the morning, just time to begin lessons: you'd only have to whisper a hint to Time, and round goes the clock in a twinkling! Half-past one, time for dinner!'

('I only wish it was,' the March Hare said to itself in a whisper.)

'That would be grand, certainly,' said Alice thoughtfully, 'but then – 'I shouldn't be hungry for it, you know.'

'Not at first, perhaps,' said the Hatter: 'but you could keep it to half-past one as long as you liked.'

'Is that the way *you* manage?' Alice asked.

The Hatter shook his head mournfully. 'Not I!' he replied. 'We

quarrelled last March – just before *he* went mad, you know –'
(pointing with his teaspoon at the March Hare,) '– it was at the
great concert given by the Queen of Hearts, and I had to sing

> "Twinkle, twinkle, little bat!
>   How I wonder what you're at!"

You know the song, perhaps?'

'I've heard something like it,' said Alice.

'It goes on, you know,' the Hatter continued, 'in this way:

> "Up above the world you fly,
>   Like a tea-tray in the sky.
>
> Twinkle, twinkle – "'

Here the Dormouse shook itself, and began singing in its sleep,
'*Twinkle, twinkle, twinkle, twinkle –*' and went on so long that they
had to pinch it to make it stop.

'Well, I'd hardly finished the first verse,' said the Hatter, 'when
the Queen bawled out "He's murdering the time! Off with his
head!"'

'How dreadfully savage!' exclaimed Alice.

'And ever since that,' the Hatter went on in a mournful tone, 'he
wo'n't do a thing I ask! It's always six o'clock now.'

—Lewis Carroll, *Alice's Adventures
in Wonderland*, 1865

*(It has been suggested that Wonderland's twelve sections follow the hours of day,
and the twelve of Looking Glass the hours of night.)*

-ᗐ ᗕ-

HESPERIAN DEPRESSION IN MAN

Normal mental pain in man, generally speaking, is tidal in character. With sunrise or during the early morning it is at its lowest ebb, to reach its highest flow in the evening about the time of the setting sun. In great cities and in the midst of strenuous civilizations it is difficult to study the nature of this tidal swing because of the infinite influences which all tend to modify the normal manifestation, and also because of the many remedies which man, when congregated in great numbers, devises to counteract the diurnal crisis. It is just when under more natural conditions the psychological process would assert itself, and become clearly apparent, that a thousand places of amusement stand out most enticingly. It is then that man, assisted by an artificial environment created, if unconsciously, nonetheless certainly to that end, can shift the centre of mental attention completely. It is not

> ... in luxurious cities, where the noise
> Of riot ascends above their loftiest towers,
> And injury, and outrage: and when night
> Darkens the streets, then wander forth the sons
> Of Belial, flown with insolence and wine
> [*Paradise Lost*, I, 496–500]

where normal Hesperian depression can best be measured and appreciated.

It is under more natural conditions, where all these artificial remedies are wanting, that this depression appears as a clearly recognizable attribute of human mentality. On the veld it is known and discussed by both Europeans and natives with the same familiarity that any other universal common mental state is recognized and discussed. It is very remarkable and interesting that the depression reaches a climax immediately after sunset and endures for a short period only. When darkness has once settled, the mental condition changes entirely. Among the natives these phases are very noticeably translated into behaviour. An air of quietness and dejection falls upon the village just about sunset. The men and women go listlessly and mournfully about such tasks as still remain to be done. The old people gather in sheltered corners or about the fireplaces, quite silent. Conversation ceases. No song is heard and no sound of musical instruments. It seems very like the dejection of utter physical weariness. [*Marais' note:* All these signs are, of course, absent in a village where beer has been made and is being drunk.] The little children are by no means exempt. All laughter ceases, the games come to an end and there is a general tendency to creep closer to the mothers and elders; an apparent craving for protective fondling and endearments. As the night falls, the scene changes. The fires are newly made. Conversation and laughter are heard once more. Songs and the sound of music arise and under the brightening stars the young people congregate at the dancing-place, where the last vestiges of dejection and weariness vanish.

It is interesting to note that here, too, there is a general tendency to describe the depression as the product of reason. The more uncivilized natives ascribe it to a fear of approaching darkness. It is during the dark hours, they suggest, that wizards go forth to create misery and distress; to sow disease and death against their defenceless neighbours. It is then that the spirits of the dead have the opportunity of manifesting themselves in a manner profoundly malevolent to the living; and other evil powers of unknown origin have all to wait for the night to attain their wicked purpose. Small wonder, therefore, they say, that human beings should become thoughtful and distressed at the time of approaching night. Why the condition should change for the better when darkness has actually arrived, they are (like their more civilized neighbours) quite unable to explain, or the explanation is childishly illogical. The Boers explain the condition, as might be expected, on more abstract grounds. The coming of night suggests the approach of death; the utter futility of human life; the distressing certainty of the end of all things; and the helplessness and paltriness of man. Of all this the setting sun is a recurring emblem.

If this state of mind is not easily recognizable in the midst of great civilizations, it must not be assumed that it is absent. In some degree it is universally expressed and has been an attribute of human mentality since the beginning of history. In the sun-stories of the dawn of civilization the daily death of the great luminary appears as typifying the feeling. In poetry and art it reappears throughout the history of human culture. No artist has fixed upon canvas the colour and light and atmosphere of this special time of day without in some measure imbuing his composition with the 'sadness that comes with the evening'. Even under the chisel of the sculptor it has found expression in every age in innumerable stones.

In religion all pronounced and common human psychological phases are represented in some form. This 'evening melancholy', which would naturally be accentuated in the religious temperament, appears magnificently in the stately formalities of both Eastern and Western Christian Churches. In all religious literature man's helplessness in the presence of an evil against which his own inward means of defence are so clearly powerless is constantly expressed:

Abide with me; fast falls the eventide ...

It is in poetry, song and music, however, that this psychological process has come to striking utterance. How many 'nocturnes' are there which owe their popularity chiefly to the profound melancholy which the artist was able to express in beautiful words, colours or tones, and which finds an instant echo in most human souls? Very often it is the powerful suggestion of death which is accepted and expressed as the cause:

The curfew tolls the knell of parting day ...

But even when it is the beauty of the evening which makes the stronger appeal, it is seldom that that beauty can be expressed without revealing its inherent melancholy. One remembers as an example of this Milton's lines from *Paradise Lost*, which Newton described as unparalleled in verse:

Now came still evening on, and twilight grey
Had in her sober livery all things clad;
Silence accompanied...
—from Eugene Marais, *The Soul of the White Ape,*
*c.*1935– 6; first published 1969

(This book is a neglected gem.)

⊰ ⊱

Six o'clock in Princes Street

In twos and threes, they have not far to roam,
    Crowds that thread eastward, gay of eyes;
Those seek no further than their quiet home,
    Wives, walking westward, slow and wise.

Neither should I go fooling over clouds,
    Following gleams unsafe, untrue,
And tiring after beauty through star-crowds,
    Dared I go side by side with you;

Or be you in the gutter where you stand,
    Pale rain-flawed phantom of the place,
With news of all the nations in your hand,
    And all their sorrows in your face.
            —Wilfred Owen (1893– 1918)

In Australia, until a final change of licensing hours in 1967: closing
time for pubs, and thus the terrifying conclusion of the so-called 'Six
O'Clock Swill', a ferocious beer binge that began, usually at about
5.30 p.m. – 'or any time after the end of work' – and accelerated
into a frantic attempt to get as much down the neck as possible in
the last few minutes. Five pints in half an hour was the standard. A
more detailed description of the required technique (beer supplies

stacked on the floor, between the feet) can be found in Keith Dunstan's novel *Wowsers*.

'The Magic Hour': in cinematography, 'the brief period between sunlight and full darkness in which shadows are long and the light has a deep, warm tone'.

Christ is brought off the cross.

> The Curfeu tolls the Knell of passing Day,
> The lowing Herd winds slowly o'er the Lea,
> The Plow-man homeward plods his weary Way,
> And leaves the World to Darkness, and to me.
>
> Now fades the glimmering Landscape on the Sight,
> And all the Air a solemn Stillness holds;
> Save where the Beetle wheels his droning Flight,
> And drowsy Tinklings lull the distant Folds.
>
> Save that from yonder Ivy-mantled Tow'r
> The mopeing Owl does to the Moon complain
> Of such, as wand'ring near her sacred Bow'r
> Molest her ancient solitary Reign.
>
> Beneath those rugged Elms, that Yew-Tree's Shade,
> Where heaves the Turf in many a mould'ring Heap,
> Each in his narrow Cell for ever laid,
> The rude Forefathers of the Hamlet sleep …
>
> —Thomas Gray, 'Elegy Wrote in a
> Country Church Yard', 1751

[Curfeu: Gray's original spelling reminds the twenty-first century of the origins of 'curfew' as 'couvre-feu'. At one time the signal for all lights and fires to be extinguished for the night, by Gray's time it referred to the tolling of the evening bell.]

Calling on Mycroft Holmes at the Diogenes Club

I had never heard of the institution, and my face must have proclaimed as much, for Sherlock Holmes pulled out his watch.

'The Diogenes Club is the queerest club in London, and Mycroft one of the queerest men. He's always there from a quarter to five till twenty to eight. It's six now, so if you care for a stroll this beautiful evening I shall be very happy to introduce you to two curiosities.'

Five minutes later we were in the street, walking towards Regent's Cross.

'You wonder,' said my companion, 'why it is that Mycroft does not use his powers for detective work. He is incapable of it.'

'But I thought you said – !'

'I said that he was my superior in observation and deduction. If the art of the detective began and ended in reasoning from an arm-chair, my brother would be the greatest criminal agent that ever lived. But he has no ambition and no energy. He would not even go out of his way to verify his own solutions, and would rather be considered wrong than take the trouble to prove himself right. Again and again I have taken a problem to him and have received an explanation which has afterwards proved to be the correct one. And yet he was absolutely incapable of working out the practical points which must be gone into before a case could be laid before a judge or jury.'

'It is not his profession, then?'

'By no means. What is to me a means of livelihood is to him the merest hobby of a dilettante. He has an extraordinary faculty for figures, and audits the books in some of the government departments. Mycroft lodges in Pall Mall, and he walks round the corner into Whitehall every morning and back every evening. From year's end to year's end he takes no other exercise, and is seen nowhere else, except only in the Diogenes Club, which is just opposite his rooms.'

'I cannot recall the name.'

'Very likely not. There are many men in London, you know, who, some from shyness, some from misanthropy, have no wish for the company of their fellows. Yet they are not averse to comfortable chairs and the latest periodicals. It is for the convenience of these that the Diogenes Club was started, and it now contains the most unsocial and most unclubbable men in town. No member is permitted to take the least notice of any other one. Save in the Stranger's Room, no talking is, under any circumstance, permitted, and three offences, if brought to the notice of the committee, render the talker liable to expulsion. My brother was one of the founders, and I have myself found it a very soothing atmosphere.'

We had reached Pall Mall as we talked, and were walking down it from the St James's end. Sherlock Holmes stopped at a door some little distance from the Carlton, and, cautioning me not to speak, he led the way into the hall. Through the glass panelling I caught a glimpse of a large and luxurious room in which a considerable number of men were sitting about and reading papers, each in his own little nook.

—Arthur Conan Doyle, 'The Greek Interpreter',
in *The Memoirs of Sherlock Holmes*, 1893

7 p.m. to 8 p.m.

Original hour of *Compline*: literally, 'Completed'.

CURTAINS UP

In most periods – since the development of appropriate indoor lighting – 7 p.m has been the usual evening opening hour for theatres in the UK, though, since the late 1940s and early 1950s 7.30 p.m. has become rather more common, except on press nights when it is brought forward to 7 p.m. to allow the critics another 30 minutes of writing time before they hurriedly file their overnight notices. There have been one or two fluctuations: in Hood's time, as we have seen, performances began at six; in the later Victorian and Edwardian periods, in response to the habit of later and later hours of dining, some theatres chose to raise their curtains at 8.15, 8.30 (the most common) or 8.45 p.m. And in the early nineteenth century it was customary for theatres to offer tickets at half price from nine onwards, to catch the crowds coming out of beer houses who did not mind seeing only the latter part of a play or spectacle.

After the First World War, the time began to creep forward again, and though there was a spirited attempt by managements after the Second World War to reinstate the 8.30 opening, the public successfully resisted, at least to the extent of the 7.30 p.m. compromise. Broadly speaking, though, when a novelist or diarist of the last three centuries refers to going to an evening performance, she or he means a show that started at seven.

Sala Goes Backstage at the Theatre

Seven o'clock post meridian has brought us at least the artificial abnegation of daylight, and has subjected us to the *régime* of gaslight. You had a twinkle of that unwholesome vapour, under the head of public dinners; but henceforth Sol will shine no longer on our labours. It is seven o'clock in the evening, and we are going to the play.

When I state that the subjects of this article are a Theatrical Green-Room, and 'Behind the Scenes', I anticipate some amount of intellectual commotion among the younger, and especially the 'fast' portion, of my readers. Jaunty young clerks, and incipient men about town, dwelling in decorous country boroughs, will be apt to fancy that I am about to launch into a deliriously exciting account of those charmed regions which lie beyond the stage-door; that my talk will be altogether of spangles, muslin skirts, and pink tights. Nay, even my young lady readers may deceive themselves with the idea that I shall draw a glowing picture of the dangerous, delightful creatures who flutter every night before theatrical audiences, and of the dear, naughty, wicked, darling marquises, earls, and baronets who lounge behind the scenes. *Hélas! il n'en est rien.* I know all about green-rooms, wings, and prompt-boxes. I have been in the artistes *foyer* of the Grand Opera, and in the mezzanine floor of the Princess's. I am not about to be cynical, but I must be prosaic, and mean to tell you, in a matter-of-fact way, what the green-room and behind the scenes of a London theatre are like at seven o'clock …

There is, the moralist hath said, a time for all things, and that much libelled institution, a theatre, has among its Bohemian faults of recklessness and improvidence, the somewhat rare virtue of punctuality. Even those events of its daily life which depend for the extent of their duration upon adventitious circumstances, are marked by a remarkably well-kept average. Theatrical rehearsals generally commence at ten o'clock in the morning; and though it will sometimes happen, in the case of new pieces about to be produced – especially pantomimes and *spectacles* – that the rehearsal is prolonged to within a few minutes of the rising of the curtain for the evening performance, the usual turning of an ordinary rehearsal's, or series of rehearsals', lane is four o'clock p.m. Then the *répétiteur* in the orchestra shuts up his fiddle in its case, and goes home to his tea. Then the young ladies of the *corps de ballet*, who have been indulging in saltatory movements for the last few hours, lay aside their 'practising dresses' – generally frocks of ordinary material, cut short in the manner immortalised by that notable pedlar, Mr Stout, in his felonious transaction with the little old woman who fell asleep by the king's highway – and subside into the long-flounced garments of common life, which are to be again replaced so soon as seven o'clock comes, by the abridged muslin skirts and flesh-coloured continuations of ballet-girlhood. The principal actresses and actors betake themselves to dow shines obliquely through the vast dimness, and rescues the kettle-drums in the orchestra from tenebrose oblivion, you might fancy this place, which two hours hence will be brilliantly lighted up, full of gorgeous decorations and blithesome music, and a gay audience shouting applause to mimes and jesters and painted bavadères, chasing the golden hours with frolic feet – you might fancy the deserted theatre to be a Valley of Dry Bones…

The theatre sleeps a sound, tranquil sleep for some hundred minutes; but at about six it begins to wake again to fresh life and activity. At half-past six it is wide open and staring. The 'dressers', male and female, have arrived, and are being objurgated by incensed performers in their several *cabinets de toilette*, because they are slow in finding Mr Lamplugh's bagwig, or Mademoiselle Follejambe's white satin shoes. The call-boy – that diminutive, weazened specimen of humanity, who has never, so it seems, been a boy, and never will be a man – has entered upon his functions, and already meditates a savage onslaught on the dressing-room doors, accompanied by a shrill intimation that the overture is 'on'…

—George Augustus Sala, *Twice Around the Clock*, 1858-9

The little painted angels flit,
  See, down the narrow staircase, where
The pink legs flicker over it!

Blonde, and bewigged, and winged with gold,
  The shining creatures of the air
Troop sadly, shivering with cold.

The gusty gaslight shoots a thin
  Sharp finger over cheeks and nose
  Rouged to the colour of the rose.

dinner, or to a walk in the park, or give themselves a finishing touch of study in the parts they are not yet quite perfect in, or, it may be, mount the steep theatrical stairs to the mountainous regions where dwell the theatrical tailor and tailoress – I entreat them to excuse me, the *costumier* and the mistress of the robes – with whom they confer on the weighty subject of the dresses which they are to wear that evening. The carpenters abandon work; the scene-shifters, whose generic name in technical theatrical parlance is 'labourers', moon about the back part of the stage, seeing that the stick of scenery for the evening is all provided, the grooves duly blackleaded and the traps greased, and all the 'sinks' and 'flies', ropes and pulleys, and other theatrical gear and tackle, in due working order. For, you see, if these little matters be not rigidly and minutely attended to, if a rope be out of its place or a screw not rightly home, such trifling accidents as mutilation and loss of life are not unlikely to happen. That the occurrence of such casualties is of so extreme a rarity may be ascribed, I think, to the microscopic care and attention which these maligned theatrical people bestow on every inch of their domain behind the scenes. They have to work in semi-darkness, and under many other circumstances of equal disadvantage; but, next to a fire engine station and the 'tween decks of a man o'war, I do not that I can call to mind a more orderly, better-disciplined tended place than that part of a theatre which lies be foot-lights ...

By five o'clock the little industries that have pre the rehearsal ended are mostly completed; and th comes quite still. It is a complete, a solemn, a stillness. All the busy life and cheerful murmi ant-hill are hushed. The rows of seats are degrees of some old ruined amphitheatre in a desert. The 'flies' and 'borders' loom indistinctness. Afar off the dusky, feeble moon on which no sun condescends to one ray of golden afternoon sunlight

All wigs and paint, they hurry in:
   Then, bid their radiant moment be
   The footlight's immortality!
        —Arthur Symons, *London Nights*,
                second edition, 1897

Pip Sees Mr Wopsle and Co. Play Hamlet

On our arrival in Denmark, we found the king and queen of that country elevated in two arm-chairs on a kitchen-table, holding a Court. The whole of the Danish nobility were in attendance; consisting of a noble boy in the wash-leather boots of a gigantic ancestor, a venerable Peer with a dirty face who seemed to have risen from the people late in life, and the Danish chivalry with a comb in its hair and a pair of white silk legs, and presenting on the whole a feminine appearance. My gifted townsman stood gloomily apart, with folded arms, and I could have wished that his curls and forehead had been more probable.

Several curious little circumstances transpired as the action proceeded. The late king of the country not only appeared to have been troubled with a cough at the time of his decease, but to have taken it with him to the tomb, and to have brought it back. The royal phantom also carried a ghostly manuscript round its truncheon, to which it had the appearance of occasionally referring, and that, too, with an air of anxiety and a tendency to lose the place of reference which were suggestive of a state of mortality. It was this, I conceive, which led to the Shade's being advised by the gallery to 'turn over!' – a recommendation which it took extremely ill. It was likewise to be noted of this majestic spirit that whereas it always appeared with an air of having been out a long time and walked an immense distance, it perceptibly came from a closely contiguous wall. This occasioned its terrors to be received derisively. The Queen of Denmark, a very buxom lady, though no doubt historically brazen, was considered by the public to have too much brass about her; her chin being attached to her diadem by a broad band of that metal (as if she had a gorgeous toothache), her waist being encircled by another, and each of her arms by another, so that she was openly mentioned as 'the kettledrum'. The noble boy in the ancestral boots, was inconsistent; representing himself, as it were in one breath, as an able seaman, a strolling actor, a grave-digger, a clergyman, and a person of the utmost importance at a Court fencing-match, on the authority of whose practised eye and nice discrimination the finest strokes were judged. This gradually led to a want of tolera-tion for him, and even – on his being detected in holy orders, and declining to perform the funeral service – to the general indignation taking the form of nuts. Lastly, Ophelia was a prey to such slow musical madness, that when, in the course of time, she had taken off her white muslin scarf, folded it up, and buried it, a sulky man who had been long cooling his impatient nose against an iron bar in the front row of the galley, growled, 'Now the baby's put to bed let's have supper!' Which, to say the least of it, was out of keeping.

Upon my unfortunate townsman all these incidents accumu-lated with playful effect. Whenever that undecided Prince had to ask a question or state a doubt, the public helped him out with it. As for example; on the question whether 'twas nobler in the mind to suffer, some roared yes, and some no, and some inclining to both opinions said 'toss up for it'; and quite a Debating Society arose. When he asked what such fellows as he do crawling between earth and heaven, he was greeted with loud cries of 'Hear, hear!' When he appeared with his stocking disordered (its disorder expressed, according to usage, by one very neat fold in the top, which I suppose to be always got up with a flat iron), a conversation took place in the gallery respecting the paleness of his leg, and whether it was occasioned by the turn the ghost had given him. On his taking the recorders – 'very like a little black flute that had just been played in the orchestra and handed out at the door' – he was called upon unanimously for Rule Britannia. When he recommended the player not to saw the air thus, the sulky man said 'And don't *you* do it, neither; you're a deal worse than *him*!' And I grieve to add that peals of laughter greeted Mr Wopsle on every one of these occasions.

But his greatest trials were in the churchyard: which had the appearance of a primeval forest, with a kind of small ecclesiastical wash-house on one side, and a turnpike gate on the other. Mr Wopsle in a comprehensive black cloak, being descried entering at the turnpike, the gravedigger was admonished in a friendly way, 'Look out! Here's the undertaker a coming, to see how you're a getting on with your work!' I believe it is well known in a constitutional country that Mr Wopsle could not possibly have returned the skull, after moralising over it, without dusting his fingers on a white napkin taken from his breast; but even that innocent and indispensable action did not pass without the comment 'Wai-ter!' The arrival of the body for interment (in an empty black box with the lid tumbling open) was the signal for a general joy which was much enhanced by the discovery, among the bearers, of an individual obnoxious to identification. The joy attended Mr Wopsle through his struggle with Laertes on the brink of the orchestra and the grave, and slackened no more until he had tumbled the king off the kitchen table, and had died by the inches from the ankles upward.

We had made some pale efforts in the beginning to applaud Mr Wopsle; but they were too hopeless to be persisted in. Therefore we had sat, feeling keenly for him, but laughing, nevertheless, from ear to ear.

—Charles Dickens, *Great Expectations*, 1860– 61

━┥ ┝━

Not everyone was drawn to the theatre at this hour.

> Now stir the fire, and close the shutters fast,
> Let fall the curtains, wheel the sofa round,

And while the bubbling and loud-hissing urn
Throws up a steamy column, and the cups
That cheer but not inebriate, wait on each,
So let us welcome peaceful evening in.
Not such his evening, who with shining face
Sweats in the crowded theatre, and, squeezed
And bored with elbow-points through both his sides,
Out scolds the ranting actor on the stage.
                              —William Cowper, *The Task*, Book IV,
                                   'The Winter Evening', 1785

[cups / That cheer: Cowper's euphemism for tea became widely repeated, and has survived to the present. He adapted it from a phrase in Siris by Bishop Berkeley, who was referring to tar-water.]

⊰ ⊱

From 7 to 7.30 p.m., Paul Fussell observes in *Class*, is the time at which the American middle classes prefer to eat their evening meal. As a general rule of thumb, he continues, the later an American family dines, the higher its class: upper-middles finally sit down at about 8 to 8.30 p.m., and the truly posh at 9 p.m. or later. It is the thoughtless habit of the nouveaux riches to dine at very late hours, thus causing the staff no end of inconvenience. American proles, he suggests, prefer to have done with their last main feed of the day at 6 to 6.30 p.m. or even earlier.

Thoreau and the Whippoorwills

Regularly at half past seven, in one part of the summer, after the evening train had gone by, the whippoorwills chanted their vespers for half an hour, sitting on a stump by my door, or upon the ridge pole of the house. They would begin to sing almost with as much precision as a clock, within five minutes of a particular time, referred to the setting of the sun, every evening.

I had a rare opportunity to become acquainted with their habits. Sometimes I heard four or five at once in different parts of the wood, by accident one a bar behind another, and so near me that I distinguished not only the cluck after each note, but often that singular buzzing sound like a fly in a spider's web, only proportionately louder. Sometimes one would circle round and round me in the woods a few feet distant as if tethered by a string, when probably I was near its eggs. They sang at intervals throughout the night, and were again as musical as ever just before and about dawn.

—Henry David Thoreau, *Walden*, 1854

Lord Byron Waits for the Clock to Strike Eight

Dined *versus* six o' the clock. Forgot that there was a plum-pudding (I have added, lately, *eating* to my 'family of vices') and had dined before I knew it. Drank half of a bottle of some sort of spirits – probably spirits of wine; for what they call brandy, rum, etc., etc., here is nothing but spirits of wine, coloured accordingly. Did *not* eat two apples, which were placed by way of dessert. Fed the two cats, the hawk, and the tame (but not tamed) crow. Read Mitford's *History of Greece* – Xenophon's *Retreat of the Ten Thousand*. Up to this present moment writing, 6 minutes before 8 o' the clock – French hours, not Italian.

Hear the carriage – order pistols and great coat – necessary articles. Weather cold – carriage open, and inhabitants rather savage – rather treacherous and highly inflamed by politics. Fine fellows though – good materials for a nation. Out of chaos God made a world, and out of high passions come a people.
Clock strikes – going out to make love. Somewhat perilous but not disagreeable. Memorandum – a new screen put up today. It is rather antique but will do with a little repair.

—Cited by W.H. Auden in *A Certain World:*
A Commonplace Book, 1971, where it is given as a
ripe example of 'Prose, Impressionistic'

╺╣ ╠╸

8 p.m. to 9 p.m.

Samuel Pepys Watches the Gamblers

1 January 1668

By and by I met with Mr Brisband, and having it in mind this Christmas to go to see the manner of the gaming at the Groome-Porter's [the Court official in charge of gaming tables], I did tell Brisband of it, and he did lead me thither: where, after staying an hour, they began to play at about eight at night, where to see how one man took his losing from another, one cursing and swearing, and another only muttering and grumbling to himself, a third without any apparent discontent at all; to see how the dice will run good luck in one hand for half an hour together, and another have no good luck at all; to see how easily here, where they play nothing but guinnys, a £100 is won or lost; to see two or three gentlemen come in there drunk, and putting their stock of gold together, one 22 pieces, the second 4, and the third 5 pieces, and these to play one with another, and forget how much each of them brought, but he that brought the 22 thinks that he brought no more than the rest; to see the different humours of gamesters to change their luck when it is bad, how ceremonious they are as to call for new dice, to shift their places, to alter their manner of throwing, and that with great industry, as if there was anything in it; to see how some old gamesters that have no money now to spend as formerly do come and sit and look on as among others, Sir Lewis Dives, who was here, and hath been a great gamester in his time; to hear their cursing and damning to no purpose, as one man being to throw a seven if he could, and failing to do it after a great many throws cried he would be damned if ever he flung seven more while he lived, his despair of throwing it being so great, while others did it as their luck served almost every throw; to see how persons of the best quality do here sit down and play with people of any, though meaner; and to see how people in ordinary clothes shall come hither and play away 100, or 2 or 300 guinnys, without any kind of difficulty; and lastly, to see the formality of the groome-porter, who is their judge of all disputes in play and all quarrels that may arise therein, and how his under-officers are there to observe true play at each table, and to give new dice, is a consideration I could never have thought had been in the world, had I not now seen it. And mighty glad I am that I did see it, and it may be will find another evening before Christmas be over to see it again, when I may stay later, for their heat of play begins not till about eleven or twelve o'clock; which did give me another pretty observation of a man, that did win mighty fast when I was there. I think he won £100 at single pieces in a little time. While all the rest envied him his good fortune he cursed it, saying, 'A pox on it, that it should come so early upon me, for this fortune two hours hence would be worth something to me, but then, God damn me, I shall have no such luck.' This kind of prophane, mad entertainment they give themselves. And so I, having enough for once, refusing to venture, though Brisband pressed me hard, and tempted me with saying that no man was ever known to lose the first time, the devil being too cunning to discourage a gamester; and he offered me also to lend me ten pieces to venture, but I did refuse, and so went away, and took coach and home about 9 or 10 at night.

—*Diaries*

Eight o'Clock

Supper comes at five o'clock,
   At six, the evening star,
My lover comes at eight o'clock –
But eight o'clock is far.

How could I bear my pain all day
   Unless I watched to see
The clock-hands labouring to bring
   Eight o'clock to me.
     —Sara Teasdale, from *Flame and Shadow,* 1924

❧ ❧

DINNER AT EIGHT

The belief that eight o'clock is the civilized hour to go in or sit down to dinner became fairly well established by about 1900, though quiet family dinners might still be held a little earlier, at about 7.30 to 7.45 p.m. Polite society on both sides of the Atlantic shared this belief. Hence 'an American Lady' (namely, Anna Steele Richardson) writes:

Q. What is the correct hour for dinner?
A. Eight o'clock in winter; half past eight in summer, unless the guests are to be taken to the theater, to the opera, or to a concert. In that case, seven fifteen or seven thirty at the latest is the correct hour.
     —*Standard Etiquette,* New York, 1925

An English Lady of almost exactly the same period (1926), Lady Troubridge, offers some very slight variations: either

7.45 ['an hour which old-fashioned people like']
or 8
or 8.15 to 8.30 ['which is the fashionable hour'].

'It is generally understood', she adds, 'that an invitation for 7.45 means that dinner will be served at 8 p.m.'

As we have noted throughout, the hour for dinner has been creeping ever later with the passing decades. In the 1850s, Arnold Palmer observes:

Thackeray makes it clear that there were already two ways of dining. When at home he dined about 6 o'clock; Dickens preferred some half an hour earlier; these seem to have been the usual and favourite hours of busy men who could eat when they wished. The meal was solid and simple, the courses few ...

As the years advanced from 1850 to 1860, Thackeray's dinner-hour moved from 6 to 6.30, to 7, then to an occasional 7.30 or even 7.45. An hour earlier, Dickens kept his distance; in 1855 we find him asking Wilkie Collins to join him at his habitual hour of 5.30, and in 1866 a similar invitation to Browning, begs him to be punctual at 6.30.

—*Movable Feasts*, 1952

The most magnificent dinner invitation in the English language was written significantly before this period, by Ben Jonson. He does not specify an hour, but clearly intended a night-time feast rather than a midday or afternoon repast.

> Tonight, grave Sir, both my poor house and I
> Do equally desire your company:
> Not that we think us worthy such a guest,
> But that your worth will dignify our feast,
> With those that come; whose grace will make that seem
> Something, which, else, could hope for no esteem.
> It is the fair acceptance, Sir, creates
> The entertainment perfect: not the cates.
> Yet you shall have, to rectify your palate,
> An olive, capers, or some better salad
> Ushering the mutton; with a short-legged hen,
> If we can get her, full of eggs, and then,
> Lemons, and wine for sauce; to these, a coney
> Is not to be despised of, for our money;
> And, though fowl, now, be scarce, yet there are clerks,
> The sky not falling, think we may have larks.
> I'll tell you of more, and lie, so you will come:

Of partridge, pheasant, wood-cock, of which some
May yet be there; and godwit, if we can:
　　Knat, rail, and ruff too. How so e'er, my man
Shall read a piece of VIRGIL, TACITUS,
　LIVY, or some better book to us,
Of which we'll speak our minds, amidst our meat;
　　And I'll profess no verses to repeat:
To this, if ought appear, which I know not of,
　　That will the pastry, not my paper, show of.
Digestive cheese, and fruit there sure will be;
　　But that, which most doth take my *Muse*, and me,
Is a pure cup of rich *Canary*-wine,
　　Which is the *Mermaid's,* now, but shall be mine:
Of which had HORACE, or ANACREON tasted,
　　Their lives, as do their lines, till now had lasted.
Tobacco, *Nectar*, or the *Thespian* spring,
　　Are all but LUTHER's beer, to this I sing.
Of this we shall sup free, but moderately,
　　And we shall have no *Pooly*, or *Parrot* by;
Nor shall our cups make any guilty men:
　　But, at our parting, we will be, as when
We innocently met. No simple word,
　　That shall be uttered at our mirthful board,
Shall make us sad next morning; or affright
　　The liberty, that we'll enjoy tonight.

[Mermaid: that is, the Mermaid Tavern]

Le Diner

Come along, 'tis the time, ten or more minutes past,
And he who came first had to wait for the last;
The oysters ere this had been in and been out;
While I have been sitting and thinking about
　　How pleasant it is to have money, heigh-ho!
　　How pleasant it is to have money.

A clear soup with eggs; *voila tout*; of the fish
The *filets de sole* are a moderate dish
A la Orly, but you're for red mullet, you say:
By the gods of good fare, who can question to-day
   How pleasant it is to have money, heigh-ho!
   How pleasant it is to have money.

After oysters, sauterne; then sherry; champagne,
Ere one bottle goes, comes another again;
Fly up, though bold cork, to the ceiling above,
And tell to our ears in the sound that they love
   How pleasant it is to have money, heigh-ho!
   How pleasant it is to have money.

I've the simplest of palates; absurd it may be,
But I almost could dine on a *poulet-au-riz*,
Fish and soup and omelette and that – but the deuce –
There were to be woodcocks, and not *Charlotte Russe!*
   So pleasant it is to have money, heigh-ho!
   So pleasant it is to have money.

Your Chablis is acid, away with the hock,
Give me the pure juice of your purple Médoc:
St Peray is exquisite; but, if you please,
Some burgundy just before tasting the cheese.
   So pleasant it is to have money, heigh-ho!
   So pleasant it is to have money.

As for that, pass the bottle, and d– n the expense,
I've seen it observed by a writer of sense,
That the labouring classes could scare live a day,
If people like us didn't eat, drink, and pay.
   So useful it is to have money, heigh-ho!
   So useful it is to have money.

One ought to be grateful, I quite apprehend,
Having dinner and supper and plenty to spend,
And so suppose now, while the things go away,
By way of a grace we all stand up and say
   How pleasant it is to have money, heigh-ho!
   How pleasant it is to have money.
               —Arthur Hugh Clough, from
                Spectator ab extra, 1850

The French Chancellor d'Aguesseau observed that his wife was habitually late coming to the dinner table, leaving him to wait for ten minutes or more. In a spirit that would have delighted Benjamin Franklin, d'Aguesseau began to write a few lines in this interval every evening. It took him little more than a year to produce a three-volume book, which became a best-seller on its publication in 1668.

-ᴤ ᴣ-

When the American Theater Guild began rehearsals for the first US run of *Saint Joan*, it was discovered that the play ran for at least three and a half hours, which meant that, if it began at the company's usual hour of 8 p.m., the final curtain would fall long past the hour when suburban playgoers could reasonably expect to catch their last trains home. They wrote to Shaw asking if he could cut the play. Shaw's reply: run later trains.

Grown Up

Was it for this I uttered prayers,
And sobbed and cursed and kicked the stairs,
That now, domestic as a plate,
I should retire at half-past eight?
       —Edna St Vincent Millay (1892– 1950)

Jonathan Harker's Journal (kept in shorthand)

2 May. Bistritz. – Left Munich at 8.35 p.m., on 1st May, arriving at Vienna early next morning; should have arrived at 6.46, but train was an hour late. Buda-Pesth seems a wonderful place, from the glimpse which I got of it from the train and the little I could walk through the streets ...

—The opening lines of Bram Stoker's *Dracula*, 1897

Stoker (*pace* A. N. Wilson's misleading introduction to the Oxford World's Classics edition of the novel) spent a great deal of time and energy researching the subjects he required for the great vampire yarn, and among his principal sources were European train timetables. In artistic terms, the deliberate mundanity of Harker's journal serves (a) to root the fantastic events to come firmly in reality, (b) to hint that Harker himself is a precise, perhaps rather too precise, young man, and (c) to underline the fact that this tale of timeless horror is going to take place in the time-bound modern world of railways.

It has also been noted that Stoker, a theatrical manager, was well used to poring over railway timetables when organizing tours for Henry Irving's company; and that, anyway, he had an abiding love for trains:

The train journeys from city to city delighted Stoker; he thrived on the strenuous schedule and the romance of the railroads. During his confined childhood, he had listened to the whistle of the Dublin-to-Drogheda train as it rumbled over the Great Northern Railway viaduct. The sound meant adventure, chance encounters, clockwork chases, scenarios he used in his novels. When Jonathan Harker enters Count Dracula's room, he finds him lying on a sofa reading – what else? – *Bradshaw's Railway Guide* ...

—Barbara Belford, *Bram Stoker*, 1996

⊰ ⊱

9 p.m. to 10 p.m.

At 9 p.m. on 18 June 1815, the Battle of Waterloo finally won, Blucher and Wellington rode forward to greet each other on the Brussels road between *La Belle-Alliance* and Rossomme. Blucher greeted him with the words: *Mein lieber Kamarad!*, and leaned forward in his saddle to kiss the Duke. *Quelle affaire!* In later years, Wellington said that this was just about all the French he knew.

A BRIEF HISTORY OF LIGHTING

As the historian William T. O'Dea observed in his classic study *The Social History of Lighting*, there was practically no improvement in the technology of light from about 15,000 BC to 1782, and the invention of the Argand lamp. The New Testament warns us that the Night cometh, wherein no man may work, and we read it solely as a *memento mori*; but for countless generations it was the literal truth, unless they sought the relatively feeble help of candles, tapers, torches, oil lamps and, eventually, the early forms of lanterns. Most great cities made at least some attempt to light their streets at night, and so put some damper on the otherwise inevitable violence and anarchy. St Jerome reported some form of lighting at crossroads in Jerusalem as early as the fourth century AD; the Arabs are reported to have paved and lit many miles of streets in Cordova during the tenth century; Paris employed a system of lamps at intersections in the thirteenth and fourteenth centuries, though this was a matter of religious observance rather than civil order.

And so on. Lighting began to improve significantly after 1750, in response to and as part of the Industrial Revolution, but the great leap forward was the Argand oil burner – safe, reliable, and capable of producing ten to twelve times as much light as conventional lamps. In the first few years of its manufacture it remained a luxury item, but was soon deployed more generally; and it was followed by, among other welcome inventions, the kerosene lamp (around 1869), and the electric filament lamp (Swan's in 1878, Edison's in 1879). These innovations changed the look of cities at night for ever, and customs changed to keep pace with them. Shops, for example, began to stay open later. (As a junior shop assistant, Robert Owen would close up his shutters at 10.30 p.m., having first opened them at 8 a.m. But his tasks were far from complete, and it was usually 2 a.m. by the time he was in bed.) And the streets themselves, once perilous for the solitary walker, became ever more safe, ever more attractive.

On the occasion of the king's birthday in 1805, and as part of a shrewd publicity campaign, the National Light and Heat Company mounted a number of gas lights along the wall of His Majesty's house in Pall Mall. Four years later, Pall Mall became the first street in the world to be lit entirely by gas. By 1823 there were 39,504 public gas lamps, lighting 215 miles of London's streets. Compare John Gay's sardonic account of hazardous noctambulism from the early eighteenth century with Richard Le Gallienne's (mostly serious) outburst of exultation, and it is hard to believe that the two writers are describing the same city.

-=| |=-

OF WALKING THE STREETS BY NIGHT

Invocation

O TRIVIA, Goddess, leave these low Abodes,
And traverse o'er the wide Ethereal Roads,
Celestial Queen, put on thy Robes of Light,
Now Cynthia nam'd, fair Regent of the Night.
At Sight of thee, the Villain sheaths his Sword,
Nor scales the Wall, to steal the wealthy Hoard.
Oh! may thy Silver Lamp in Heav'n's high Bow'r
Direct my Footsteps in the Midnight Hour.

[In its singular form, the Latin 'trivium' meant 'crossroads' or, more exactly, 'meeting of three roads.' In its plural, 'trivia', it usually meant 'the public streets'.]

The Evening

When Night first bids the twinkling Stars appear,
Or with her cloudy Vest inwraps the Air,
Then swarms the busie Street; with Caution tread,
Where the Shop-Windows falling threat thy Head;
Now Lab'rers home return, and join their Strength
To bear the tott'ring Plank, or Ladder's Length;
Still fix thy Eyes intent upon the Throng,
And as the Passes open, wind along...

[vest: robe; passes: bottle-necks in the city streets]

The Danger of Crossing a Square by Night

Where Lincoln's-Inn, wide Space, is rail'd around,
Cross not with vent'rous Step: there oft' is found
The lurking Thief, who while the Day-light shone,
Made the Walls eccho with his begging Tone:
That Crutch which late Compassion mov'd, shall wound
Thy bleeding Head, and fell thee to the Ground.
Though thou art tempted by the Link-man's Call,
Yet trust him not along the lonely Wall;
In the Mid-way he'll quench the flaming Brand,
And share the Booty with the pilf'ring Band.
Still keep the publick Streets, where oily Rays,
Shot from the Crystal Lamp, o'erspread the Ways.

[link-man: a professional torch-bearer, who would light pedestrians' ways for a fee; oily rays: from the 1690s onwards, London's main streets were lit at night by oil lamps with thick glass panes]

Of Oysters

Be sure observe where brown Ostrea stands,
Who boasts her shelly Ware from Wallfleet Sands;
There may'st thou pass, with safe unmiry Feet,
Where the rais'd Pavement leads athwart the Street.
If where Fleet-Ditch with muddy Current flows,
You chance to roam; where Oyster-Tubs in Rows
Are rang'd beside the Posts; there stay thy Haste,
And with the sav'ry Fish indulge thy Taste:
The Damsel's Knife the gaping Shell commands,
While the salt Liquor streams between her Hands.

That Man had sure a Palate cover'd o'er
With Brass or Steel, that on the rocky Shore
First broke the oozy Oyster's pearly Coat,
And risqu'd the living Morsel down his Throat.
What will not Luxury taste? Earth, Sea and Air
Are daily ransack'd for the Bill of Fare.
Blood stuff'd in Skins is British Christian's Food,
And France robs Marshes of the croaking Brood;
Spungy Morells in strong Ragousts are found
And in the Soupe the slimy Snail is drown'd.

[ostrea: the oyster-woman; blood stuff'd: Gay refers, of course, to Black Pudding. Though Gay's poem is not well known as a whole, this section is often cited in cookery books and the like.]

How to Know a Whore

'Tis She who nightly strolls with saunt'ring Pace,
No stubborn Stays her yielding Shape embrace;
Beneath the Lamp her tawdry Ribbons glare,
The new-scower'd Manteau, and the slattern Air;

High-draggled Petticoats her Travels show,
And hollow Cheeks with artful Blushes glow;
With flatt'ring Sounds she sooths the cred'lous ear,
My noble Captain! Charmer! Love! my Dear!
In Riding-hood, near Tavern-Doors she plies,
Or muffled Pinners hide her livid Eyes.
With empty Bandbox she delights to range,
And feigns a distant Errand from the Change;
Nay, she will oft' the Quaker's Hood prophane,
And trudge demure the Rounds of Drury-Lane.
She darts from Sarsnet Ambush wily Leers,
Twitches thy Sleeve, or with familiar Airs,
Her Fan will pat thy Cheek; these Snares disdain,
Nor gaze behind thee, when she turns again.

*[new-scower'd Manteau: i.e. a newly washed – because second-hand – gown;
high-draggled: splashed with mud well above the ankles, and thus proof that she
has been walking the streets as no proper Lady would; Riding-hood: like that
worn by the fairy-tale heroine, a hood that completely covers the head, like a
monk's cowl; muffled Pinners: a type of headdress with hanging flaps, to conceal
the marks of venereal disease and the like on the prostitute's face; Sarsnet:
sarsenet, a fine material often used for lining hoods]*

A Dreadful Example

I knew a Yeoman, who for thirst of Gain,
To the great City drove from Devon's Plain
His num'rous lowing Herd; his Herds he sold,
And his deep leathern Pocket bagg'd with Gold;
Drawn by a fraudful Nymph, he gaz'd, he sigh'd;
Unmindful of his home, and distant Bride,
She leads the willing Victim to his Doom,
Through winding Alleys to her Cobweb Room.
Thence thro' the streets he reels, from Post to Post,
Valiant with Wine, nor knows his Treasure lost.

The vagrant Wretch th' assembled Watchmen spies,
He waves his Hanger, and their Poles defies;
Deep in the Round-House pent, all Night he snores,
And the next Morn in vain his Fate deplores.

Ah hapless Swain, unus'd to Pains and Ills!
Canst thou forgo Roast-Beef for nauseous Pills?
How wilt thou lift to Heav'n thy Eyes and Hands,
When the long Scroll the Surgeon's Fees demands!
Or else (ye Gods avert that worst Disgrace)
Thy ruin'd nose falls level with thy Face,
Then shalt thy Wife thy loathsome Kiss disdain,
And wholesome Neighbours from thy Mug refrain.

[Hanger: a short sword; Poles: the staves issued to the watchmen; Round-House: a small lock-up, used for overnight detention of prisoners; forgo Roast-Beef: it was believed that those in treatment for venereal disease should avoid 'heating' foods like beef; Mug: literally, that they would not wish to drink from the same cup, but with the punning implication that they would recoil from his disfigured face]

Of Rakes

Now is the Time that Rakes their Revells keep;
Kindlers of Riot, Enemies of Sleep.
His scatter'd Pence the flying Nicker flings,
And with the Copper Shower the Casement rings.
Who has not heard the Scowrer's Midnight Fame?
Who has not trembled at the Mohock's Name?
Was there a Watchman took his hourly Rounds,
Safe from their Blows, or new-invented Wounds?

[Nicker: Gay himself explained that this was a type of hooligan 'who delighted to break windows with Half-pence'. Nicker, Scowrer and Mohock are all names *for assorted street gangs, often made up of young men from wealthy families, who plagued London at the time. 'Mohock' is a corrupted form of 'Mohawk'.]*

—Extracted from John Gay's mock-epic *Trivia*,
Book III , first published in 1714

A Ballad of London

Ah, London! London! our delight,
Great flower that opens but at night,
Great City of the Midnight Sun,
Whose day begins when day is done.

Lamp after lamp against the sky
Opens a sudden beaming eye,
Leaping alight on either hand,
The iron lilies of the Strand.

Like dragonflies, the hansoms hover,
With jewelled eyes, to catch the lover;
The streets are full of lights and loves,
Soft gowns, and flutter of soiled doves.

The human moths about the light
Dash and cling close in dazed delight,
And burn and laugh, the world and wife,
For this is London, this is life! ...

—Richard Le Gallienne, 1895

Boswell is Propositioned

Wednesday, 3 August 1763

I should have mentioned that on Monday night, coming up the Strand, I was tapped on the shoulder by a fine fresh lass. I went home with her. She was an officer's daughter, and born at

Gibraltar. I could not resist indulging myself with enjoyment of her. Surely, in such a situation, when the woman is already abandoned, the crime must be alleviated, though in strict morality, illicit love is always wrong.

—*London Diaries*

-⟨ ⟩-

In the UK 9 p.m. is the so-called 'watershed' hour for broadcasting – the hour, that is, by which it is assumed that smaller children will be tucked up safely in bed, and the television channels are at greater liberty to show violent news footage or drama, discuss or portray sexual acts, and use profane language.

Dover Beach

The sea is calm to-night.
The tide is full, the moon lies fair
Upon the straits; on the French coast the light
Gleams and is gone; the cliffs of England stand,
Glimmering and vast, out in the tranquil bay.
Come to the window, sweet is the night-air!
Only, from the long line of spray
Where the sea meets the moon-blanched land,
Listen! you hear the grating roar
Of pebbles which the waves draw up, and fling,
At their return, up the high strand,
Begin, and cease, and then again begin,
With tremulous cadence slow, and bring
The eternal note of sadness in.

Sophocles long ago
Heard it on the Aegean, and it brought
Into his mind the turbid ebb and flow

Of human misery; we
Find also in the sound a thought,
Hearing it by this distant northern sea.

The Sea of Faith
Was once, too, at the full, and round earth's shore
Lay like the folds of a bright girdle furled.
But now I only hear
Its melancholy, long, withdrawing roar,
Retreating, to the breath
Of the night-wind, down the vast edges drear
And naked shingles of the world.

Ah, love, let us be true
To one another! for the world, which seems
To lie before us like a land of dreams,
So various, so beautiful, so new,
Hath really neither joy, nor love, nor light,
Nor certitude, nor peace, nor help for pain;
And we are here as on a darkling plain
Swept with confused alarms of struggle and flight,
Where ignorant armies clash by night.

—Matthew Arnold, probably *c.* June 1851

Glum Evenings at the Brontë Parsonage

[It is the winter of 1836:] It was the household custom among the
girls to sew until 9 o'clock at night. When their duties for the day
were accounted done, they put away their work and began to
pace backwards and forwards, up and down – as often with the
candles extinguished for economy's sake as not – their figures
glancing into the firelight and out into the shadow, perpetually.

—Mrs Gaskell, *The Life of Charlotte Brontë*, 1857

For many years under British law, 9 p.m. was the hour at which the offence of housebreaking became the far more serious crime of burglary. If the criminal had the patience to wait all night until 6 a.m., his crime would revert to mere housebreaking again. Incidentally, marriage without a special licence became a crime at 6 p.m. but legal again at 8 a.m.

Wemmick Fires the Nine o'Clock Cannon

[Pip is being shown around Wemmick's eccentric house and grounds.]

'At nine o'clock every night, Greenwich time,' said Wemmick, 'the gun fires. There he is, you see! And when you hear him go, I think you'll say he's a Stinger!'

The piece of ordnance referred to, was mounted in a separate fortress, constructed of lattice-work. It was protected from the weather by an ingenious little tarpaulin contrivance in the nature of an umbrella...

[Pip takes punch with Wemmick while his father, the Aged Parent, potters around in the garden. The hour approaches.]

The punch being very nice, we sat there drinking it and talking, until it was almost nine o'clock. 'Getting near gun-fire,' said Wemmick then, as he laid down his pipe; 'it's the Aged's treat.' Proceeding into the Castle again, we found the Aged heating the poker, with expectant eyes, as a preliminary to the performance of this great nightly ceremony. Wemmick stood with his watch in his hand, until the moment was come for him to take the red-hot poker from the Aged, and repair to the battery. He took it, and went out, and presently the Stinger went off with a Bang that shook the crazy little box of a cottage as if it must fall to pieces, and made every glass and teacup in it ring. Upon this, the Aged – who I believe would have been blown out of his arm-chair but for holding on by the elbows – cried out exult-

ingly, 'He's fired! I heerd him!', and I nodded at the old gentleman until it is no figure of speech to declare that I absolutely
could not see him.

—Charles Dickens, *Great Expectations*, 1860–61

⊰ ⊱

In winter at nine, and in summer at ten,
To bed after supper, both ladies and men.
                    —Thomas Tusser, *Five Hundred Points*
                              of Good Husbandry, 1571)

Sitting Alone on an Autumn Night
I sit alone sad at my whitening hair
Waiting for ten o'clock in my empty house
In the rain the hill fruits fall
Under my lamp grasshoppers sound
White hairs will never be transformed
That elixir is beyond creation
To eliminate decrepitude
Study the absolute.

                    —Wang Wei (AD 699–761),
                         trans. G. W. Robertson

⊰ ⊱

10 p.m. to 11 p.m.

Pepys Fears His Night Walk Home

21 August 1665

I was forced to walk it in the dark, at 10 a-clock at night, with Sir
J. Mennes's George with me – being mightily troubled for fear

of the Dogs at Coome farme, and more for fear of rogues by way, and yet more because of the plague which is there (which is very strange, it being a single house, all alone from the town; but it seems they use to admit beggars (for their own safety) to lie in their barns, and they brought it to them); but I bless God, I got about 11 of the clock well to my wife; and giving 4s. [shillings] in recompense to George, I to my wife; and having first viewed her last piece of drawing since I saw her (which is seven or eight days), which pleases me beyond anything in the world, I to bed with great content – but weary.

—Diaries

Sala, Lamenting Poor Town Planning, Heads for a Political Debate

I wend my way at Ten o'Clock at night along the New Road – what do they call it now? Euston Road, Pancras Road, Paddington Road – *que scais-je* – towards the suburban district of Pentonville. It won't be suburban much longer; for Clerkenwell and Islington, Somers Town and Finsbury, are hemming it in so closely that it will be engulphed some of these days by a brick-and-mortar torrent, like the first Eddystone Lighthouse. A pleasant spot once was Pentonville, haunted by cheery memories of Sir Hugh Myddleton, the New River Head, Sadlers' Wells Theatre, and the 'Angel' at Islington – which isn't (at least now-a-days, and I doubt if it ever was) at Islington at all. They began to spoil Pentonville when they pulled down that outrageously comic statue of George IV, at Battle Bridge. Then they built the Great Northern Railway Terminus – clincher number one; then an advertising tailor built a parody of the Crystal Palace for a shop – clincher number two (I am using a Swivellerism). The pre-ordinate clincher had been the erection of the hideously lugubrious penitentiary. However, I suppose it is all for the best. The next step will be to brick up the reservoir, and take down that mysterious tuning-fork looking erection, which no doubt has something to do with the water supply of London, and the

New River Head; then they had better turn the Angel into a select vestry-room or a meeting-house for the Board of Works; and then, after that, I should advise them to demolish the 'Belvidere'.

... At this famous and commodious old tavern, one of the few in London that yet preserve, not only a local but a metropolitan reputation, there is held every Saturday evening – ten o'clock being about the time for the commencement of the mimic Wittenagemotte – one of those meetings for political discussion, and the 'ventilation' of political questions, whose uninterfered-with occurrence, not only here, but in Fleet Street, in Bride Lane, and in Leicester Square, so much did rouse the ire of the *sbirri*, and *mouchards*, and unutterable villainy of Rue de Jerusalem spydom, in the employ of his Imperial Majesty, Napoleon III.

—George Augustus Sala, *Twice Round the Clock*, 1858– 9

In his fascinating study of Baudelaire, Walter Benjamin noted that, at the heyday of the Second Empire in Paris, the shops in the main streets did not close before ten o'clock at night. 'It was,' Benjamin observes, 'the great period of *noctambulisme* ...', and he refers his readers to Delvau's *Heures Parisiennes* of 1866.

> Wee Willie Winkie rins through the town,
> Up stairs and doon stairs in his nicht-gown,
> Tirling at the window, crying at the lock,
> 'Are the weans in their beds, for it's now ten o'clock?'
> —William Miller, 'Willie Winkie'

-☃ ☃-

NIGHT LIFE

At the Cavour

Wine, the red coals, the flaring gas,
Bring out a brighter tone in cheeks

That learn at home before the glass
    The flush that eloquently speaks.

The blue-grey smoke of cigarettes
    Curls from the lessening ends that glow;
The men are thinking of the bets,
    The women of the debts, they owe.
Then their eyes meet, and in their eyes
    The accustomed smile comes up to call,
A look half miserably wise,
    Half heedlessly ironical.
            —Arthur Symons, *Silhouettes*,
            2nd edition, 1896

Jerome K Jerome Sups In Style

[The hour is 10.30 p.m.:]

I must confess to enjoying that supper. For about ten days we seemed to have been living, more or less, on nothing but cold meat, cake, and bread and jam. It had been a simple, a nutritious diet; but there had been nothing exciting about it, and the odour of Burgundy, and the smell of French sauces, and the sight of clean napkins and long loaves, knocked as a very welcome visitor at the door of our inner man.

We pegged and quaffed away in silence for a while, until the time came when, instead of sitting bolt upright, and grasping the knife and fork firmly, we leant back in our chairs and worked slowly and carelessly – when we stretched out our legs beneath the table, let our napkins fall, unheeded, to the floor, and found time to more critically examine the smoky ceiling than we had hitherto been able to do – when we rested our glasses at arm's length upon the table, and felt good, and thoughtful, and forgiving.
            —Jerome K. Jerome, *Three Men in a Boat*, 1889

-=┨ ┠-

CAROUSING

[The narrator is an Englishman, recently arrived in Istanbul:]

Eventually we reached a café where I was to be shown off as the latest capture. One drink after another was put in front of me. Relays of food appeared with dreadful regularity. It was very typical Turkish hospitality. They take a great pleasure and pride in entertaining and very often a competition develops. You have only to mention a dish and it is summoned for trial. It is impossible (and rude) to buy things in return.

I became fuller and tighter, lost badly at whist and backgammon, defeated them in an argument about the Koran, sang some Irish songs and, Celtic abandonment conquering Saxon decorum, swore allegiance with the peoples of Islam. Abdul did an acrobatic stunt with some chairs and this was followed by a cockroach race over twenty feet.

The cockroach, which most people find so repulsive, is really, as Fabre pointed out, quite a pleasant creature – but obstinate. Shining magnificently in their black armour, their antennae wavering uncertainly, they were coaxed into starting positions. There were a dozen runners with a man on his hands and knees behind each one. Once they were going they moved at a great pace.

It was like being in Dublin again. The drinks came – green, amber and red: crème de menthe, beer and wine; then *raki* to complete the demolition. I had not drunk so much for months. I felt the years fall away, dissolve, with each new drink. Good resolutions, the doctor's advice, the minatory nibbling of an ulcer, the occasional stammer in the heart – all the obstructions of restraint and good sense and self-abnegation dispersed.

As the cockroaches were returned to the gutter I remembered that I had, the next morning, to go and see some newly revealed mosaics, but even as I remembered it I knew it would not be an appointment that I would be able to keep.

Finally, so I was assured a week later, I attempted at their behest to teach them the rudiments of cricket in the cafe, which was cleared for the purpose, and promised very foolishly to turn out for the local soccer team the following Saturday. It was a memorable evening – in so far as it could be remembered. Long before, in 1571, Ouloudji Ali took refuge in the harbour of Tersane with the remains of his fleet which had been defeated by John of Austria at Lepanto – that battle in which Cervantes lost an arm. Afterwards, the Sultan, Selim II, lay prostrate on the ground for three days and would not eat anything. I lay prostrate for one day and could not eat anything.

—J. A. Cuddon, *The Owl's Watchsong*, 1960

EARLY CLOSING

In eighteenth-century Scotland, closing time in inns was marked by the drinkers being 'drummed out' – usually at 10 p.m. – by the municipal drum.

But when the lower orders stop drinking, the upper classes may begin: Lady Laura Troubridge (1926) notes that 'Evening Parties' are to be held between 10 p.m. and midnight.

Pascal's Vision

Pascal's *Memorial* of 1654 is a profoundly moving document, which commemorates a period of some two hours in which the great mathematician and religious thinker underwent a direct experience of Divine Grace. He is said to have kept a copy of this text stitched into his clothes for the rest of his life.

The year of grace 1654.
Monday, 23 November, feast of Saint Clement, Pope and Martyr, and of others in the Martyrology.

Eve of Saint Chrysogonus, Martyr and others.
From about half past ten in the evening until half past midnight.

Fire

'God of Abraham, God of Isaac, God of Jacob,'[1]
not of philosophers and scholars.
Certainty, certainty, heartfelt, joy, peace.
God of Jesus Christ.
God of Jesus Christ.
My God and your God.[2]
'Thy God shall be my God.'[3]
The world forgotten, and everything except God.
He can only be found by the ways taught in the Gospels.
Greatness of the human soul.

'O righteous Father, the world had not known thee, but I have
known thee.'[4]
Joy, joy, joy, tears of joy.
I have cut myself off from him.
They have forsaken me, the fountain of living waters.[5]
'My God wilt thou forsake me?'[6]
Let me not be cut off from him for ever!
'And this is life eternal, that they might now thee, the only true God,
and Jesus Christ whom thou hast sent.'[7]
Jesus Christ.
Jesus Christ.
I have cut myself off from him, shunned him, denied him,
crucified him.
Let me never be cut off from him!
He can only be kept by the ways taught in the Gospel.
Sweet and total renunciation.
Total submission to Jesus Christ and my director.
Everlasting joy in return for one day's effort on earth.
I will not forget thy word.[8] Amen.

Notes:
1. Exodus 3:6.
2. John 20:17.
3. Ruth 1:16.
4. John 17:25.
5. Jeremiah 2:13.
6. Cf. Matthew 27:46.
7. John 17: 3.
8. Psalms 119:16.

⊰⊱

11 p.m. to Midnight

AND SO TO BED

Elegie: To his Mistris Going to Bed

Come, Madame, come, all rest my powers defie,
Until I labour, I in labour lye.
The foe oft-times, having the foe in sight,
Is tir'd with standing, though they never fight.
Off with that girdle, like heavens zone glistering
But a farre fairer world encompassing.
Unpin that spangled brest-plate, which you weare
That th'eyes of busy fooles may be stopt there:
Unlace your self, for that harmonious chime
Tells me from you that now 'tis your bed time.
Off with that happy buske, whom I envye
That still can be, and still can stand so nigh.
Your gownes going off such beauteous state reveales
As when from flowery meades th' hills shadow steales.
Off with your wyrie coronet and showe
The hairy dyadem which on you doth growe.
Off with those shoes: and then safely tread

In this loves hallow'd temple, this soft bed.
In such white robes heavens Angels us'd to bee
Receiv'd by men; Thou Angel bring'st with thee
A heaven like Mahomets Paradise; and though
Ill spirits walk in white, we easily know
By this these Angels from an evill sprite:
They set our haires, but these the flesh upright.

   License my roving hands, and let them goe
Behind, before, above, between, below.
Oh my America, my new found lande,
My kingdome, safeliest when with one man man'd,
My mine of precious stones, my Empiree,
How blest am I in this discovering thee.
To enter in these bonds is to be free,
Then where my hand is set my seal shall be.

   Full nakednesse, all joyes are due to thee.
As souls unbodied, bodies uncloth'd must be
To taste whole joyes. Gems which you women use
Are as Atlanta's balls, cast in men's viewes,
That when a fooles eye lighteth on a gem
His earthly soule may covet theirs not them.
Like pictures, or like bookes gay coverings made
For laymen, are all women thus arraid;
Themselves are mystique bookes, which only wee
Whom their imputed grace will dignify
Must see reveal'd. Then since I may knowe,
As liberally as to a midwife showe
Thy selfe; cast all, yea this white linnen hence.
There is no penance due to innocence.

   To teach thee, I am naked first: Why then
What need'st thou have more covering than a man.
                —John Donne, first published in *Poems*, 1669

⊰⊱

But the Quincunx of Heaven runs low, and tis time to close the five ports of knowledge; We are unwilling to spin out our awaking thoughts into the phantasmes of sleep, which often continueth praecogitations; making Cables of Cobwebbes, and Wildernesses of handsome Groves. Besides *Hippocrates* hath spoke so little, and the Oneirocriticall Masters, have left such frigid Interpretations from Plants, that there is little encouragement to dream of Paradise itself. Nor will the sweetest delight of Gardens afford much comfort in sleep; wherein the dulnesse of that sense shakes hands with delectable odours; and though in the Bed of *Cleopatra*, can hardly with any delight raise up the ghost of a Rose.

Night which Pagan Theology could make the daughter of Chaos, affords no advantage to the description of order: Although no lower than that Masse can we derive its Genealogy. All things begin in order, so shall they end, and so shall they begin again; according to the ordainer of order and mystical Mathematics of the City of Heaven.

Though Somnus in Homer be sent to raise up *Agamemnon*, I finde no such effects in these drowsy approaches of sleep. To keep our eyes open longer were but to act our Antipodes. The huntsmen are up in *America*, and they are already past their first sleep in *Persia*. But who can be drowsie at that hour which freed us from everlasting sleep? Or have slumbering thoughts at that time, when sleep itself must end, and as some conjecture all shall wake again.

—Sir Thomas Browne, *The Garden of Cyrus*, 1658

ON THE DOOMSDAY CLOCK

In 1947, the Board of Directors of the American *Bulletin of the Atomic Scientists* devised the symbol of the 'Doomsday Clock', a simple graphic to indicate how close the world might be to a nuclear war: the clock is set at X minutes to midnight, and the minute hand is moved forward as the state of international tension increases. Initially set at seven minutes to midnight, the hand moved backwards and forwards throughout the Cold War, but has been less jittery since 1991.

The outlook is not as optimistic as this may suggest, however: on 27 February 2002, the clock was moved forward to … seven minutes to midnight.

(On 17 January 2007, as this book was going to press, the BAS announced that it had moved the hands of the clock forward two minutes, in view of the increasingly dangerous state of global politics. For the time being we are five minutes to midnight.)

LAST ORDERS

11.00 p.m.: today, the most common closing time for pubs in the United Kingdom. The modern history of opening and closing times, as most drinkers will knowingly tell you, begins with DORA, the Defence of the Realm Act, passed during the First World War. It was introduced, so the story goes, to limit the effect of hangovers among workers in munitions factories – though the modern legal regulation of drinking times in the United Kingdom actually begins in the early 1870s. The phrase – and some of its near relatives ('Time, Gentlemen, Please…', 'Hurry up, please, it's time…') – has considerable force as a metaphor, as was noticed by T. S. Eliot in Book Two of *The Waste Land*, by the Canadian song-writer Leonard Cohen in his track of that name, and by Cyril Connolly:

'It is closing time in the Gardens of the West, and from now on an artist will be judged only by the resonance of his solitude or the quality of his despair'.
            —Editorial in the last issue of *Horizon*, November 1949

No wonder stars are winking,
    No wonder heaven mocks
At men who cease from drinking
    Good booze because of clocks!

It makes me wonder whether
In this grim pantomime
Did fiend or man first blether:
'Time, Gentlemen, Time!'
—Oliver St John Gogarty

⊰ ⊱

Gibbon's Farewell to
The Decline and Fall of the Roman Empire

It was on the day, or rather night, of the 27th of June, 1787, between the hours of eleven and twelve, that I wrote the last lines of the last page, in a summer-house in my garden. After laying down my pen, I took several turns in a *berceau*, or covered walk of acacias, which commands a prospect of the country, the lake, and the mountains. The air was temperate, the sky was serene, the silver orb of the moon was reflected from the waters, and all nature was silent. I will not dissemble the first emotions of joy on the recovery of my freedom, and, perhaps, the establishment of my fame. But my pride was soon humbled, and a sober melancholy was spread over my mind, by the idea that I had taken an everlasting leave of an old and agreeable companion, and that whatsoever might be the future date of my History, the life of the historian must be short and precarious.   —*Memoirs*, 1796

'The eleventh hour': the source of this phrase is the Parable of the Workers in the Vineyard (Matthew 20:1– 14).

For the kingdom of heaven is like unto a man that is an householder, which went out early in the morning to hire labourers into his vineyard.

And when he had agreed with the labourers for a penny a day, he sent them into his vineyard.

And he went out about the third hour, and saw others standing idle in the marketplace,

And said unto them; Go ye also into the vineyard, and whatsoever is right I will give you. And they went their way.

Again he went out about the sixth and ninth hour, and did likewise.

And about the eleventh hour he went out, and found others standing idle, and saith unto them, Why stand ye here all the day idle?

They say unto him, Because no man hath hired us. He saith unto them, Go ye also into the vineyard; and whatsoever is right, that shall ye receive.

So when even was come, the lord of the vineyard saith unto his steward, Call the labourers, and give them their hire, beginning from the last unto the first.

And when they came that were hired about the eleventh hour, they received every man a penny.

But when the first came, they supposed that they should have received more; and they likewise received every man a penny.

And when they had received it, they murmured against the goodman of the house,

Saying, these last have wrought but one hour, and thou hast made them equal unto us, which have borne the burden and the heat of the day.

But he answered one of them, and said, Friend, I do thee no wrong: didst not thou agree with me for a penny?

Take that thine is, and go thy way: I will give unto this last, even as unto thee.

The cryptic title of Ruskin's great tract on political economy, *Unto This Last* (1860– 62), is taken from the same passage.

11.45 p.m., 10 May 1942: 1,048 British bombers, manned by 6,000 crew, and launched from fifty-three airfields, began dropping their bombs on Cologne. This was the first of the so-called Thousand

Bomber raids, devised by Air Marshall Harris. Despite the astonishing scale of the resulting firestorm, which destroyed well over 13,000 houses, civilian casualties were surprisingly slight: fewer than 500 dead.

The Devil Claims His Due

[The clock strikes eleven.]

FAUSTUS:

Ah, Faustus
Now hast thou but one bare hour to live,
And then thou must be damn'd perpetually.
Stand still, you ever-moving spheres of heaven,
That time may cease, and midnight never come;
Fair nature's eye, rise, rise again, and make
Perpetual day; or let this hour be but
A year, a month, a week, a natural day,
That Faustus may repent and save his soul.
O lente lente currite noctis equi!
The stars move still, time runs, the clock will strike,
The devil will come, and Faustus must be damn'd.
O, I'll leap up to my God! Who pulls me down?
See, see where Christ's blood streams in the firmament!
One drop would save my soul, half a drop. Ah, my Christ! –
Rend not my heart for naming of my Christ;
Yet will I call on him. O, spare me, Lucifer! –
Where is it now? 'Tis gone: and see where God
Stretcheth out his arm and bends his ireful brows.
Mountains and hills, come, come, and fall on me,
And hide me from the heavy wrath of God!
No, no:
Then will I headlong run into the earth.
Earth, gape! O, no, it will not harbour me.
You stars that reign'd at my nativity,
Whose influence hath allotted death and hell,

Now draw up Faustus like a foggy mist
Into the entrails of yon labouring cloud,
That, when you vomit forth into the air,
My limbs may issue from your smoky mouths,
So that my soul may but ascend to heaven.

[*The watch strikes.*]

Ah, half the hour is pass'd: 'twill all be pass'd anon.
O God,
If thou wilt not have mercy on my soul,
Yet for Christ's sake, whose blood hath ransom'd me,
Impose some end to my incessant pain;
Let Faustus live in hell a thousand years,
A hundred thousand, and at last be sav'd.
O, no end is limited to damned souls.
Why wert thou not a creature wanting soul?
Or why is this immortal that thou hast?
Ah, Pythagoras's *metempsychosis*, were that true,
This soul should fly from me and I be chang'd
Unto some brutish beast: all beasts are happy,
For when they die
Their souls are soon dissolv'd in elements;
But mine must live still to be plagu'd in hell.
Curs'd be the parents that engender'd me!
No, Faustus, curse thyself, curse Lucifer
That hath depriv'd thee of the joys of heaven.

[*The clock striketh twelve.*]

O, it strikes, it strikes! Now, body, turn to air,
Or Lucifer will bear thee quick to hell!

[*Thunder and lightning.*]

O soul, be chang'd into little water drops,
And fall into the ocean, ne'er be found.

[*Enter* DEVILS.]

My God, my God! Look not so fierce on me!
Adders and serpents, let me breathe awhile!
Ugly hell, gape not! Come not, Lucifer;
I'll burn my books! – Ah, Mephistopheles!

[*Exeunt.*]
—Marlowe, *Doctor Faustus*, V.ii

⊰ ⊱

FALSTAFF: We have heard the chimes at midnight, Master Shallow.
—*2 Henry IV*, III.ii

Envoi

So we'll go no more a-roving
   So late into the night,
Though the heart be still as loving,
   And the moon be still as bright.

For the sword outwears its sheath,
   And the soul wears out the breast,
And the heart must pause to breath,
   And Love itself have rest.

Though the night was made for loving,
   And the day returns too soon,
Yet we'll go no more a-roving
   By the light of the moon.

—Byron (1788– 1824)

(Despite the deliciously elegiac tone, the author was in fact only twenty-nine.)

Hours Four: Midnight to 6 a.m.

Midnight to 1 a.m.

[John Aubrey Encounters a Pagan Remain]

The last summer, on the eve of St John the Baptist 1694, I accidentally was walking in the pasture behind Montague House, it was 12 o'clock. I saw there about two or three and twenty young women, most of them well habited, on their knees very busy, as if they had been weeding. I could not presently learn what the matter was; at last a young man told me, that they were looking for a coal under the root of a plantain, to put under their head that night, and they should dream who would be their husbands: It was to be sought for that day and hour.

—J. Aubrey, *Miscellanies*

Frost at Midnight

The frost performs its secret ministry,
Unhelped by any wind. The owlet's cry
Came loud – and, hark, again! loud as before.
The inmates of my cottage, all at rest,
Have left me to that solitude, which suits
Abstruser musings: save that at my side
My cradled infant slumbers peacefully.
'Tis calm indeed! so calm, that it disturbs
And vexes meditation with its strange
And extreme silentness. Sea, hill, and wood,
This populous village! Sea, and hill, and wood,

With all the numberless goings on of life,
Inaudible as dreams! the thin blue flame
Lies on my low burnt fire, and quivers not;
Only that film, which fluttered on the grate,
Still flutters there, the sole unquiet thing.
Methinks, its motion in this hush of nature
Gives it dim sympathies with me who live,
Making it a companionable form,
Whose puny flaps and freaks the idling Spirit
By its own moods interprets, every where
Echo or mirror seeking of itself,
And makes a toy of Thought.

But O! how oft,
How oft, at school, with most believing mind,
Presageful, have I gazed upon the bars,
To watch that fluttering stranger! and as oft
With unclosed lids, already had I dreamt
Of my sweet birth-place, and the old church-tower,
Whose bells, the poor man's only music, rang
From morn to evening, all the hot Fair-day,
So sweetly, that they stirred and haunted me
With a wild pleasure, falling on mine ear
Most like articulate sounds of things to come!
So gazed I, till the soothing sounds I dreamt
Lulled me to sleep, and sleep prolonged my dreams!
And so I brooded all the following morn,
Awed by the stern preceptor's face, mine eye
Fixed with mock study on the swimming book:
Save if the door half opened, and I snatched
A hasty glance, and still my heart leaped up,
For still I hoped to see the stranger's face,
Townsman, or aunt, or sister more beloved,
My play-mate when we both were clothed alike!

Dear Babe, that sleepest cradled by my side,
Whose gentle breathings, heard in this deep calm,
Fill up the interspersed vacancies
And momentary pauses of the thought!
My babe so beautiful! it thrills my heart
With tender gladness, thus to look at thee,
And think that thou shalt learn far other lore
And in far other scenes! For I was reared
In the great city, pent 'mid cloisters dim,
And saw nought lovely but the sky and stars.
But thou, my babe! shalt wander like a breeze
By lakes and sandy shores, beneath the crags
Of ancient mountain, and beneath the clouds,
Which image in their bulk both lakes and shores
And mountain crags: so shalt thou see and hear
The lovely shapes and sounds intelligible
Of that eternal language, which thy God
Utters, who from eternity doth teach
Himself in all, and all things in himself.
Great universal Teacher! he shall mould
Thy spirit, and by giving make it ask.

Therefore all seasons shall be sweet to thee,
Whether the summer clothe the general earth
With greenness, or the redbreast sit and sing
Betwixt the tufts of snow on the bare branch
Of mossy apple-tree, while the nigh thatch
Smokes in the sun-thaw; whether the eve-drops fall
Heard only in the trances of the blast,
Or if the secret ministry of frost
Shall hang them up in silent icicles,
Quietly shining to the quiet Moon.
                    —Samuel Taylor Coleridge (1772– 1834)

(Written in February 1798, and first published later that year. The village is

Nether Stowey, and the infant Hartley Coleridge. The poet explained the slightly cryptic reference to the 'film' by noting: 'In all parts of the kingdom these films are called strangers and supposed to portend the arrival of some absent friend.' He revised and cut the poem several times; this text follows the edition of 1834.)

Rain

Rain, midnight rain, nothing but the wild rain
On this bleak hut, and solitude, and me
Remembering again that I shall die
And neither hear the rain nor give it thanks
For washing me cleaner than I have been
Since I was born into this solitude.
Blessed are the dead that the rain rains upon:
But here I pray that none whom I once loved
Is dying tonight or lying still awake
Solitary, listening to the rain,
Either in pain or thus in sympathy
Helpless among the living and the dead,
Like a cold water among broken reeds,
Myriads of broken reeds all still and stiff,
Like me who have no love which this wild rain
Has not dissolved except the love of death,
If love it be towards what is perfect and
Cannot, the tempest tells me, disappoint.
                    —Edward Thomas, 1878–1917

᠃ ᠄

THE SUPERNATURAL REPUTATION OF MIDNIGHT

'Tis now the very witching time of night,
When churchyards yawn, and Hell itself breathes out
Contagion to this world. Now could I drink hot blood,

And do such bitter business as the day
Would quake to look on ...

—*Hamlet*, III.ii

Almost every culture acknowledges that midnight is the 'witching hour' – a time when, as Hamlet suggests, demons, ghosts or fairies are prowling just beyond our fire-lights; when the wall between the living and the dead is at its thinnest and most permeable; when visions are most likely and spells most potent. Here are a few samples:

Once upon a midnight dreary,
While I pondered, weak and weary,
Over many a quaint and curious volume of forgotten lore ...

—Edgar Allan Poe, 'The Raven', 1845

HAMLET: What hour now?
HORATIO: I think it lacks of twelve.
MARCELLUS: No, it is struck.
HORATIO: Indeed I heard it not: then it draws near the season,
                        Wherein the spirit held his wont to walk ...

—*Hamlet*, I.i

THESEUS:
The iron tongue of midnight hath told twelve.
Lovers, to bed; 'tis almost fairy time.
I fear we shall outsleep the coming morn
As much as we this night have overwatch'd.
This palpable-gross play hath well beguil'd
The heavy gate of night. Sweet friends, to bed.
A fortnight hold we this solemnity
In nightly revels and new jollity.

[*Exeunt. Enter Puck.*]

PUCK:

Now the hungry lion roars,
And the wolf behowls the moon;
Whilst the heavy ploughman snores,
All with weary task fordone.
Now the wasted brands do glow,
Whilst the screech-owl, screeching loud,
Puts the wretch that lies in woe
In remembrance of a shroud.
Now it is the time of night
That the graves, all gaping wide,
Every one lets forth his sprite
In the church-way paths to glide.
And we fairies, that do run
By the triple Hecate's team
From the presence of the sun,
Following darkness like a dream,
Now are frolic; not a mouse
Shall disturb this hallow'd house.
I am sent with broom before
To sweep the dust behind the door...
—*A Midsummer Night's Dream*, V.i, *c.*1595– 6

In Russian folklore, there is a demon peculiar to midnight: the *polunosh-nik*, which preys on small children – or, in milder versions of the tale, keeps them awake. See W. F. Ryan's *The Bathhouse at Midnight: Magic in Russia*, 1999.

※ ❧

A NOCTURNAL UPON ST LUCY'S DAY,
BEING THE SHORTEST DAY

'Tis the year's midnight, and it is the day's,
Lucy's, who scarce seven hours herself unmasks;
The sun is spent, and now his flasks
Send forth light squibs, no constant rays;
The world's whole sap is sunk;
The general balm the hydroptic earth hath drunk,
Whither, as to the bed's-feet, life is shrunk,
Dead and interr'd; yet all these seem to laugh,
Compared to me, who am their epitaph …

Study me then, you who shall lovers be
At the next world, that is, at the next Spring:
For I am every dead thing,
In whom love wrought new alchemy.
For his art did express
A quintessence even from nothingness,
From dull privations, and lean emptiness:
He ruin'd me, and I am re-begot
Of absence, darkness, death; things which are not.

All others, from all things, draw all that's good,
Life, soul, form, spirit, whence they being have;
I, by love's limbeck, am the grave
Of all that's nothing. Oft a flood
Have we two wept, and so
Drown'd the whole world, us two; oft did we grow
To be two Chaoses, when we did show
Care to aught else; and often absences
Withdrew our souls, and made us carcasses.

But I am by her death (which word wrongs her),
Of the first nothing the Elixir grown;
Were I a man, that I were one
I needs must know; I should prefer,
If I were any beast,
Some ends, some means; yea plants, yea stones, detest,
And love; all, all, some properties invest;
If I an ordinary nothing were,
As shadow, a light and body must be here.

But I am none; nor will my Sun renew.
You lovers, for whose sake the lesser sun
At this time to the Goat is run
To fetch new lust, and give it you,
Enjoy your summer all:
Since she enjoys her long night's festival,
Let me prepare towards her, and let me call
This hour her Vigil, and her Eve, since this
Both the year's, and the day's deep midnight is.
                    —John Donne, written *c*.1611– 12?

(According to the Julian calendar, or so Donne appears to believe, St Lucy's day, 13 December, was the shortest day in the year. It was not.)

Midnight.

Now is the sun withdrawn into his bedchamber, the windows of heaven are shut up, and silence with darkness have made a walk over the whole earth, and time is tasked to work upon the worst actions: yet virtue being herself, is never weary of well doing, while the best spirits are studying for the body's rest; dreams and visions are the haunters of troubled spirits, while nature is most comforted in the hope of the morning: the body now lies as a dead lump, while sleep, the pride of ease, lulls the

senses of the slothful: the tired limbs now cease from their labours, and the studious brains give over their business: the bed is now an image of the grave, and the prayer of the faithful makes the pathway to Heaven: lovers now enclose a mutual content, while gracious minds have no wicked imaginations; thieves, wolves and foxes now fall to their prey, but a strong lock and a good wit will aware much mischief; and he that trusteth in God will be safe from the Devil. Farewell.

—Nicholas Breton, *The Fantasticks*, 1626

In mediaeval monasteries, midnight is usually the hour of the longest service, Matins.

Extract from a Little-Known Play

THE DEVIL:
[*Going to the timepiece.*]

Half after midnight! these mute moralizers,
Pointing to the unheeded lapse of hours,
Become a tacit eloquent reproach
Unto the dissipation of this Earth.
There is a clock in Pandaemonium,
Hard by the burning throne of my great grandsire,
The slow vibrations of whose pendulum,
With click–clack alternation to and fro,
Sound '*Ever, Never*' thro' the courts of Hell,
Piercing the wrung ears of the damned that writhe
Upon their beds of flame, and whenso'er
There may be short cessation of their wails,
Through all the boundless depth of fires is heard
The shrill and solemn warning '*Ever, Never*':
Then bitterly, I trow, they turn and toss
And shriek and shout to drown the thrilling noise.

[*Looking again at the timepiece.*]

Half after midnight! Wherefore stand I here?
Methinks my tongue runs twenty knots an hour:
I must unto mine office.
                                        [*Exit abruptly.*]

—Alfred Tennyson, aged fourteen, from
Tennyson, a Memoir, by Hallam,
Lord Tennyson, 1897

⊰ ⊱

The Bell-Man

Along the dark, and silent night,
With my Lantern, and my Light,
And the tinkling of my Bell,
Thus I walk, and this I tell:
Death and dreadfulnesse call on,
To the gen'rall Session;
To whose dismall Barre, we there
All accompts must come to cleere;
Scores of sins w'ave made here many,
Wip't out few (God knowes) if any.
Rise ye Debters then, and fall
To make payment, while I call.
Ponder this, when I am gone;
By the clock 'tis almost *One*.
                    —Robert Herrick, *His Noble Numbers*, 1647

⤙ ⤚

1 a.m. to 2 a.m.

LATE CAROUSING

Eleven – twelve – one o'clock had struck, and the gentlemen had not arrived. Consternation sat on every face. Could they have been waylaid and robbed? Should they send men and lanterns in every direction by which they could be supposed likely to have travelled home? or should they – Hark! there they were. What could have made them so late? A strange voice, too! To whom could it belong? They rushed into the kitchen whither the truants had repaired, and at once obtained rather more than a glimmering of the real state of the case.

Mr Pickwick, with his hands in his pockets and his hat cocked completely over his left eye, was leaning against the dresser, shaking his head from side to side, and producing a constant succession of the blandest and most benevolent smiles without being moved thereunto by any discernible cause or pretence whatsoever; old Mr Wardle, with a highly-inflamed countenance, was grasping the hand of a strange gentleman muttering protestations of eternal friendship; Mr Winkle, supporting himself by the eight-day clock, was feebly invoking destruction upon the head of any member of the family who should suggest the propriety of his retiring for the night; and Mr Snodgrass had sunk into a chair, with an expression of the most abject and hopeless misery that the human mind can imagine, portrayed in every lineament of his expressive face.

'Is anything the matter?' inquired the three ladies.

'Nothing the matter,' replied Mr Pickwick. 'We – we're – all right. – I say, Wardle, we're all right, an't we?'

'I should think so,' replied the jolly host. 'My dears, here's my friend, Mr Jingle – Mr Pickwick's friend, Mr Jingle, come 'pon – little visit.'

'Is anything the matter with Mr Snodgrass, sir?' inquired Emily, with great anxiety.

'Nothing the matter, ma'am,' replied the stranger. 'Cricket dinner – glorious party – capital songs – old port – claret – good – very good – wine, ma'am – wine.'

'It wasn't the wine,' murmured Mr Snodgrass, in a broken voice. 'It was the salmon.' (Somehow or other, it never *is* the wine, in these cases.)

—Charles Dickens, *The Pickwick Papers*

-ᴋᴅ ᴅᴋ-

According to Théophile Gautier, as reported in the journals of the Goncourt brothers for 14 September 1863, George Sand liked to do most of her writing between the hours of midnight and 4 a.m. On one occasion, however, she found – 'Good heavens!' – that she had finished a novel by 1 a.m. So she promptly began writing another.

Alfred Hitchcock was in the habit of falling asleep at parties. His wife Alma once woke him up when he had been asleep in the middle of noisy festivities for at least four hours. The great director looked at his watch, and replied, 'But it's only one o'clock! They'll think we aren't enjoying ourselves!'

BIG BEN

The famous chime of Big Ben is taken from that of Great St Mary's Church in Cambridge. The tune was selected by a Dr Jowett and a Mr Crotch, and comes from Handel's *Messiah*: 'I know that my Redeemer liveth.' It was borrowed for Big Ben by Lord Grimthorpe, and became known as the Westminster Chime, though knowing circles in Cambridge may still refer to it as 'Jowett's Jig'.

A popular version of the tune has imagined the accompanying text as:

> All through this hour
> Lord be my guide
> And by thy power
> No foot shall slide.

As children used to know, each of the major bells of London's churches had a song of its own: '"Oranges and Lemons" sing the bells of St Clement's ...'.

One of the clock

It is now the first hour and time is, as it were, stepping out of darkness and stealing towards the day: the cock calls to his hen and bids her beware of the fox, and the watch, having walked the streets, take a nap upon a stall: the bell-man calls to the maids to look to their locks, their fires and their light, and the child in the cradle calls to the nurse for a dug: the cat sits watching behind the cupboard for a mouse, and the flea sucks on sweet flesh, till he is ready to burst with blood: the sprits of the studious start out of their dreams, and if they cannot fall asleep again, then to the book and the wax candle: the dog at the door frays the thief from the house, and the thief within the house may hap to be about his business. In some places bells are rung to certain orders: but the quiet sleeper never tells the clock. Not to dwell too long upon it, I hold it the farewell of the night and the forerunner to the day, the spirit's watch and reason's workmaster. Farewell.

— Nicholas Breton, *The Fantasticks*, 1626

[*A Une Heure du Matin*]

Enfin! Seul! On n'entend plus que le roulement de quelques fiacres attardés et éreintés. Pendant quelques heures, nous posséderons le silence, sinon le repos. Enfin! La tyrannie de la face humaine a disparu, et je ne souffrirai plus que par moi-même.

Enfin! Il m'est donc permis de me délasser dans un bain de ténèbres! D'abord, un double tour à la serrure. Il me semble que ce tour de clef augmentera ma solitude et fortifiera les barricades qui me séparent actuellement du monde.

Horrible vie! Horrible ville! Récapitulons la journée: avoir vu plusieurs hommes de lettres, dont l'un m'a demandé si l'on pouvait aller en Russie par voie de terre (il prenait sans doute la Russie pour une île); avoir disputé généreusement contre le directeur d'une revue, qui à chaque objection répondait: 'C'est ici le parti des honnêtes gens', ce qui implique que tous les autres journaux sont rédigés par des coquins; avoir salué une vintaigne de personnes, dont quinze me sont inconnues; avoir distribué des poignées de main dans la même proportion, et cela sans avoir pris la précaution d'acheter des gants; être monté pour tuer le temps, pendant une averse, chez une sauteuse qui m'a prié de lui dessiner un costume de Vénustre; avoir fait ma cour à un directeur de théâtre, qui m'a dit en me congédiant: 'Vous feriez peut-être bien de vous addresser à Z...; c'est le plus lourd, le plus sot, et le plus célèbre de tous mes auteurs; avec lui vous pourriez peut-être aboutir à quelque chose. Voyez-le, et puis nous verrons'; m'être vanté (pourquoi?) de plusieurs vilaines actions que je n'ai jamias commises, et avoir lâchement nié quelques autres méfaits que j'ai accomplis avec joie, délit de fanfaronnade, crime de respect humain; avoir refusé à un ami un service facile, et donné une recommandation à une parfait drôle; ouf! Est-ce bien fini?

Mécontent de tous et mécontent de moi, je voudrais bien me racheter et m'enorgueillir un peu dans le silence et la solitude de la nuit. Ames de ceux que j'ai aimés, âmes de ceux que j'ai chantés, fortifiez-moi, soutenez-moi, éloignez de moi le mensonge et les vapeurs corruptrices du monde; et vous, Seigneur mon Dieu! Accordez-moi la grâce de produire quelques beaux vers qui me prouvent à moi-même que je ne suis pas la dernier des hommes, que je ne suis pas inférieur à ceux que je méprise.

— Charles Baudelaire, published August 1862

[At last! Alone! You can't hear anything but the clatter of a few late-night, worn-out cabs. For a few hours, at least we'll have silence, if not proper rest. At last! The tyranny of the human face has vanished,

and the only person to give me pain will be myself. At last! I'm allowed
to wallow in a bath of darkness! First, let's turn the key twice. It seems
to me as if this turn of the key will add to my solitude, and strengthen
the barricades that are presently dividing me from the world.

Rotten life! Rotten town! Let's run through the day: saw a few men
of letters, one of whom asked me if it was possible to travel to Russia
by land (no doubt he thought Russia was an island); had a shouting
match with the editor of a review, who to my every objection answered
'we stand up for decent people', so implying that all the other papers
are turned out by low-lifes; greeted twenty-odd individuals, of whom
fifteen were quite unknown to me; shook the same number of hands,
without having taken the precaution of buying gloves; went to visit a
dancing-girl, to kill time during a shower – she asked me to draw her
a 'Venustre' costume; dropped by to see a theatre manager, who said,
as he shuffled me out: 'You might do well to go and see M. Bloggs ... ;
he's the most sluggish, stupid and famous of all my playwrights; with him,
you could really go places. Have a word with him, and then we'll see';
bragged (why?) about a few nasty tricks I've never pulled off, and denied,
from pure cowardice, a few shabby acts that I carried out with real pleasure
– the sin of exhibitionism, a crime against human decency; refused a friend
some help that would have cost me next to nothing, and wrote a glowing
reference for a complete idiot. Whew, is that the lot?

Tired of everything, tired of myself, I would gladly look for redemp-
tion and a little restored pride in the silence and solitude of the night.
O souls of those I have loved, souls of those I have sung, strengthen me,
support me, drive from me all the lies and the corrupting vapours of the
world; and you, Lord my God! Grant me the grace to produce a few
fine lines of verse that will let me prove to myself that I am not the
lowest of men, that I am not inferior to those I despise.]

'Tis past one o'clock in the morning. I sat down at twelve o'clock
to read the 'Robbers' of Schiller. I had read, chill and trembling,
when I came to the part where the Moor fixes a pistol over the
robbers who are asleep. I could read no more. My God, Southey,
who is this Schiller, this convulser of the heart? Did he write his

tragedy amid the yelling of fiends? I should not like to be able to describe such characters. I tremble like an aspen leaf. Upon my soul, I write to you because I am frightened. I had better go to bed.

—Coleridge to Southey, November 1794

-≼ ≽-

ON DREAMS

[An early behaviourist account:]

And seeing dreams are caused by the distemper of some of the inward parts of the body, divers distempers must needs cause different dreams. And hence it is that lying cold breedeth dreams of fear, and raiseth the thoughts and image of some fearful object, the motion from the brain to the inner parts and from the inner parts to the brain being reciprocal; and that as anger causeth heat in some parts of the body when we are awake, so when we sleep the overheating of the same parts causeth anger, and raiseth up in the brain the imagination of an enemy. In the same manner, as natural kindness, when we are awake, causeth desire, and desire makes heat in certain other parts of the body; so also too much heat in those parts, while we sleep, raiseth in the brain an imagination of some kindness shown. In sum, our dreams are the reverse of our waking imaginations; the motion when we are awake beginning at one end, and when we dream at another.

—Thomas Hobbes, *Leviathan*, 1651

Methought I saw my late espoused Saint
  Brought to me like Alcestis from the grave,
  Whom Jove's great son to her glad husband gave,
  Rescued from death by force, though pale and faint.
Mine, as whom washt from spot of child-bed taint
  Purification in the old Law did save,
  And such, as yet once more I trust to have

Full sight of her in Heaven without restraint,
Came vested all in white, pure as her mind.
  Her face was veiled; yet to my fancied sight
  Love, sweetness, goodness in her person shined
So clear, as in no face with more delight.
  But O as to embrace me she inclined,
  I waked, she fled, and day brought back my night.
              — John Milton, 'On His Deceased Wife', *c.*1655

It is certain enough ... that dreams in general proceed from indigestion; and it appears nearly as much so, that they are more or less strange according to the waking fancy of the dreamer. It is probable that a trivial degree of indigestion will give rise to very fantastic dreams in a fanciful mind; while, on the other hand, a good orthodox repletion is necessary towards a fanciful creation in a dull one. It shall make an epicure, of any vivacity, act as many parts in his sleep as a tragedian, 'for that night only'. The inspirations of veal, in particular, are accounted extremely Delphic; Italian pickles partake of the same spirit of Dante; and a butter-boat shall contain as many ghosts as Charon's.
              —Leigh Hunt, 'Of Dreams', 1820

There is ... a sort of profundity in sleep; and it may be usefully consulted as an oracle ... It may be said, that the voluntary power is suspended, and things come upon us as unexpected revelations, which we keep out of our thoughts at other times. We may be aware of a danger, that yet we do not chuse, while we have the full command of our faculties, to acknowledge to ourselves: the impending event will then appear to us as a dream, and we shall most likely find it verified afterwards. Another thing of no small consequence is, that we may sometimes discover our tacit, and almost unconscious sentiments, with respect to persons or things in the same way. We are not hypocrites in our sleep. The curb is taken off from our passions, and our imagination wanders at will. When awake, we check these rising thoughts, and fancy we have them not. In dreams, we are off our guard, they return securely and unbidden. We may make this use of the infirmity of our sleeping metamorphosis, that we may repress any feelings of this sort that we disapprove in their incipient state, and detect, ere it be too late, an unwarrantable antipathy or fatal passion. Infants cannot disguise their thoughts from others; and in sleep we reveal the secret to ourselves.

—William Hazlitt, from *The Plain Speaker*, 1826

Mayakovsky's final poem:

Past One O'Clock

Past one o'clock. You must have gone to bed.
Night's Milky Way flows like a silver stream.
No rush. I'll not wake you, bothering your head
With lightning telegrams to crush your dream.
As they say, that's the end of the story,
The boat of love has smashed against life's reefs.
We are quits and we don't need an inventory
Of our mutual hurtings, insults and griefs.
And see how the world lies in quietness
The sky pays Night with a rash of stars from its purse.
In hours like this, one gets up to address
All Time and History and the Universe!

—Translation from *Modern Russian Poetry*,
editing by Vladimir Markov and
Merill Sparks, 1966

(The text of this poem was found in Mayakovsky's pocket after his suicide in 1930.)

Just before 2 a.m. on the night after the execution of Charles I, so legend has it, a dark figure with its head covered in a cowl entered the banqueting hall of Whitehall, where the monarch's remains were laid out. Those keeping vigil – including the Earl of Southampton – could not see the face of this strange man, but they heard him sigh 'Cruel necessity' before he shuffled off into the darkness. Both the voice and the gait, they reported, were those of Oliver Cromwell.

The tradition, charming though it is, is not confirmed by the more reliable sources, which say that Charles's body was taken to the embalmer's immediately after beheading.

2 a.m. to 3 a.m.

ON DAYLIGHT SAVING

'And lastly let us salute the compulsive genius of British statesmen who confronted the sun in his march and rolled back the onset of night.'

—Sir (then Mr) Winston Churchill, on the
Daylight Saving Act

0200 hrs – to be exact, 0200 hours on Sunday – is the hour at the heart of daylight saving. The scheme was first devised by William Willett, Esq. (1857– 1915), a successful London builder. Mr Willett, a keen golfer and horseman, was often given to reflect how sad it was that more people could not share his enjoyment of the early morning sunshine as he rode through Petts Woods (his home) and over Chislehurst Common in the summer months; and how annoying it was, at the same time of year, to be forced to abandon the golf links at 8 p.m. or so because of fading light. He toyed with various possibilities – including the scheme of shifting the clocks forward or backwards by twenty minutes on four successive weekends – until he came up with the proposals he set forth in a self-financed publication, *The Waste of Daylight*, in July 1907:

> Everyone appreciates the long light evenings. Everyone laments their shrinkage as the days grow shorter, and nearly everyone has given utterance to a regret that the clear bright light of early mornings, during Spring and Summer months, is so seldom seen or used…

The proposal was met with almost universal ridicule, especially by the Press: 'Will the chickens know what time to go to bed?' and so on. But Willett continued to agitate, found supporters, and within two years a Daylight Saving Bill had been drafted. The matter was dropped for a while when war broke out in 1914, but in 1916 the government passed the bill as a wartime measure of economy. Willett, alas, had died the previous year; but the residents of Petts Wood and Orpington gave him a handsome memorial in the form of a sundial, which is positioned so as to read one hour in advance of the time on an ordinary sundial. In 1925 the emergency bill was made law.

Two of the clock

It is now the second hour and the point of the dial hath stepped over the first stroke, and now time begins to draw back the curtain of the night: the cock again calls to his hen, and the watch begin to bustle toward their discharge: the bell-man hath made a great part of his walk, and the nurse begins to huggle the child to the dug; the cat sits playing with the mouse which she hath catched, and the dog with his barking wakes the servants of the house; the studious now are near upon waking, and the thief will be gone, for fear of being taken: the foresters now be about their walks, and yet stealers sometimes cozen the keepers: warreners now begin to draw homeward, and far dwellers will be on the way to the market: the soldier now looks towards the *cour de garde*, and the corporal takes care for the

relief of the watch: the earnest scholar will now be at his book, and the thrifty husbandman will rouse towards his rising: the seaman will now look out for light, and if the wind be fair, he calls for a can of beer: the fisherman now take the benefit of the tide, and he that bobs for eels will not be without worms. In sum, I hold it much to the nature of the first hour, but somewhat better. And to conclude, I think it the enemy of sleep and the entrance to exercise. Farewell.

— Nicholas Breton, *The Fantasticks*, 1626

James Boswell is Caught in the Dark

About two o'clock in the morning I inadvertently snuffed out my candle, and as my fire before that was long before black and cold, I was in a great dilemma how to proceed. Downstairs did I softly and silently step to the kitchen. But, alas, there was as little fire there as upon the icy mountains of Greenland. With a tinder box a light is struck every morning to kindle the fire, which is put out at night. But this tinder box I could not see, nor knew where to find. I was now filled with gloomy ideas of the terrors of the night. I was also apprehensive that my landlord, who always keeps a pair of loaded pistols by him, might fire at me as a thief. I went up to my room, sat quietly until I heard the watchman calling 'past three o'clock'. I then called to him to knock at the door of the house where I lodged. He did so, and I opened to him and got my candle re-lumed without danger. Thus was I relieved and continued busy until eight the next day.

—From Boswell's *London Journal*, 1762– 3

✦

ON NIGHTMARES

When I say, My bed shall comfort me, my couch shall ease my complaint; then thou scarest me with dreams, and terrifiest me through visions: so that my soul chooseth strangling, and death rather than life.

—Job 7

My dreams were of the most terrific description. Every species of calamity and horror befell me. Among other miseries, I was smothered to death between huge pillows, by demons of the most ghastly and ferocious aspect. Immense serpents held me in their embrace, and looked earnestly in my face with their fearfully shining eyes. Then deserts, limitless, and of the most forlorn and awe-inspiring character, spread themselves out before me. Immensely tall trunks of trees, gray and lifeless, rose up in endless succession as far as the eye could reach. Their roots were concealed in widespreading morasses, whose dreary water lay intensely black, still, and altogether terrible, beneath. And the strange trees seemed endowed with a human vitality, and waving to and fro their skeleton arms, were crying to the silent waters for mercy, in the shrill and piercing accents of the most acute agony and despair.

—Edgar Allan Poe, *The Narrative of Arthur Gordon Pym of Nantucket*, 1838

I remembered I was lying in the oak closet, and I heard distinctly the gusty wind, and the driving of the snow; I heard, also, the fir-bough repeat its teasing sound, and ascribed it to the right cause: but it annoyed me so much, that I resolved to silence it, if possible; and I thought, I rose and endeavoured to unhasp the casement. The hook was soldered into the staple: a circumstance observed by me when awake, but forgotten. 'I must stop it, nevertheless!' I muttered, knocking my fingers through the glass, and stretching an arm out to seize the importunate branch; instead of which, my fingers closed on the fingers of a little, ice-cold hand! The intense horror of nightmare came over me: I tried to draw back my arm, but the hand clung to it, and a most melancholy voice sobbed, 'Let me in – let me in!' 'Who are you?' I asked, struggling, meanwhile, to disengage myself. 'Cath-erine Linton,' it replied shiveringly (why did I think of *Linton*? I had read *Earnshaw* twenty times for Linton). 'I'm come home: I'd lost my way on the moor!' As it spoke, I discerned, obscurely, a child's face looking through the window. Terror made me cruel; and, finding it useless to attempt shaking the creature off, I pulled its wrist on to the broken pane, and rubbed it to and fro till the blood ran down and soaked the bedclothes: still it wailed 'Let me in!' and maintained its tenacious gripe, almost maddening me with fear. 'How can I!' I said at length. 'Let *me* go, if you want me to let you in!' The fingers relaxed, I snatched mine through the hole, hurriedly piled up the books in a pyramid against it, and stopped my ears to exclude the lamentable prayer. I seemed to keep them closed above a quarter of an hour; yet, the instant I listened again, there was the doleful cry moaning on! 'Begone!' I shouted, 'I'll never let you in, not if you beg for twenty years.' 'It is twenty years,' mourned the voice: 'twenty years. I've been a waif for twenty years!' Thereat began a fearful scratching outside, and the pile of books moved as if thrust forward. I tried to jump; but could not stir a limb; and so yelled aloud, in a frenzy of fright.

—Emily Bronte, *Wuthering Heights*, 1847

Nightmare

When you're lying awake with a dismal headache
    and repose is taboo'd by anxiety,
I conceive you may use any language you choose to
    indulge in, without impropriety;
For your brain is on fire – the bedclothes conspire of
    usual slumber to plunder you;
First your counterpane goes, and uncovers your toes,
    and your sheet slips demurely from under you;
Then the blanketing tickles – you feel like mixed
    pickles – so terribly sharp is the pricking,
And you're hot, and you're cross, and you tumble

and toss till there's nothing 'twixt you and the
ticking.
Then the bedclothes all creep to the ground in a heap,
and you pick 'em all up in a tangle;
Next your pillow resigns and politely declines to
remain at its usual angle!
Well, you get some repose in the form of a doze, with
hot eye-balls and head ever aching,
But your slumbering teems with such horrible dreams
that you'd very much sooner be waking...
—W. S. Gilbert, from *Iolanthe*

He was from a child an ardent and uncomfortable dreamer. When he had a touch of fever at night, and the room swelled and shrank, and his clothes, hanging on a nail, now loomed up instant to the bigness of a church, and now drew away into a horror of infinite distance and infinite littleness, the poor soul was very well aware of what must follow, and struggled hard against the approaches of that slumber which was the beginning of sorrows. But his struggles were in vain; sooner or later the night-hag would have him by the throat, and pluck him, strangling and screaming, from his sleep. His dreams were at times commonplace enough, at times very strange, at times they were almost formless: he would be haunted, for instance, by nothing more definite than a certain hue of brown, which he did not mind in the least while he was awake, but feared and loathed while he was dreaming; at times, again, they took on every detail of circumstance, as when once he supposed he must swallow the populous world, and awoke screaming with the horror of the thought. The two chief troubles of his very narrow existence – the practical and everyday struggle of school tasks and the ultimate and airy one of hell and judgment – were often confounded together into one appalling nightmare. He seemed to himself to stand before the Great White Throne; he was called on, poor little devil, to recite some form of words, on which his destiny depended; his

tongue stuck, his memory was blank, hell gaped for him; and he
would awake, clinging to the curtain rod with his knee to his chin.
—Robert Louis Stevenson, 'A Chapter on Dreams', 1892

(The 'he' in this passage is Stevenson himself.)

3 a.m. to 4 a.m.

ON INSOMNIA AND NIGHT HORRORS

In *The Crack-Up*, F. Scott Fitzgerald observes that for those passing
through the true Dark Night of the Soul, it is always 3 a.m. A young
poet of the twenty-first century echoes Fitzgerald's sentiment:

> Our world turns concave,
> it is 3 a.m. 24/7. Maybe
> it will feel the way it does
> when you don't recognise words,
> even though you spell them out
> the way you always have.
>
> I imagine orange groves breaking
> through the ice
> and Eskimos wandering around
> with dazed smiles and
> sweet, juice-filled mouths.
>
> —Anna Lea, *Beneath,* 2004

Cyril Connolly writes about the state of nocturnal despair both in
Enemies of Promise – at quite agonizing length – and in his classic of
melancholic introspection, *The Unquiet Grave:*

1 a.m.: Anger turns to Misery. 2 a.m.: Misery to Panic. The low tide and nadir of hope about 2. a.m. to 4. Magical Euphoria wells from 4 a.m. to 6 – the thalamic 'All Clear'; Peace and Certainty arrive through Despair. All morning the tide of confidence rolls in with the high water of egotism from 2 p.m. to 3. (We are farthest then from the idea of death as in the nocturnal small hours we are nearest.) Momentary depression at sunset, though often at my best from 6 o'clock to 10. Then the bilges begin to empty.

Some other outstanding evocations of insomnia:

> Care-charmer sleep, son of the sable night,
>   Brother to death, in silent darkness borne;
> Relieve my languish, and restore the light,
>   With dark forgetting of my care's return.
>   And let the day be long enough to mourn
> The shipwreck of my ill-adventured youth:
>   Let waking eyes suffice to wail their scorn,
> Without the torment of the night's untruth.
> Cease, dreams, th'images of day desires,
>   To model forth the passions of the morrow:
> Never let rising Sun approve you liars,
>   To add more grief to aggravate my sorrow,
> Still let me sleep, embracing clouds in vain,
> And never wake to feel the day's disdain.
>   —Samuel Daniel (1562– 1619)

I wake and feel the fell of dark, not day.
What hours, O what black hours we have spent
This night! what sights you, heart, saw; ways you went!
And more must, in yet longer light's delay.
    With witness I speak this. But where I say
Hours I mean years, mean life. And my lament
Is cries countless, cries like dead letters sent
To dearest him that lives alas! away.

I am gall, I am heartburn. God's most deep decree
Bitter would have me taste: my taste was me;
Bones built in me, flesh filled, blood brimmed the curse.
    Selfyeast of spirit a dull dough sours. I see
The lost are like this, and their scourge to be
As I am mine, their sweating selves; but worse.

—Gerard Manley Hopkins (1844– 89)

(The text was discovered after his death. It was probably written some time in August or September 1885, at about the same time as 'To seem the stranger lies my lot', 'Patience, hard thing!' and 'My own heart let me have more pity on'.)

Charles Lamb Recalls his Youthful Fear of the Dark

I was dreadfully alive to nervous terrors. The night-time solitude, and the dark, were my hell. I never laid my head on my pillow, I suppose, from the fourth to the seventh or eighth year of my life – so far as memory serves in things so long ago – without an assurance, which realised its own prophecy, of seeing some frightful spectre. Be old Stackhouse then acquitted in part, if I say, that to his picture of the Witch raising up Samuel – (O that old man covered with a mantle!) I owe – not my midnight terrors, the hell of my infancy – but the shape and manner of their visitation. It was he who dressed up for me a hag that nightly sate upon my pillow – a sure bedfellow, when my aunt or my maid was far from me. All day long, while the book was permitted to me, I dreamed waking over his delineation, and at night (if I may use so bold an expression) awoke into sleep, and found the vision true. I durst not, even in the daylight, once enter the chamber where I slept, without my face turned to the window, aversely from the bed where my witch-ridden pillow was. – Parents do not know what they do when they leave tender babes alone to go to sleep in the dark. The feeling about for a friendly arm – the hoping for a familiar voice – when they wake screaming – and find none to soothe them – what a terrible shaking it is to their poor nerves! The keeping them up till midnight, through candle-light and the unwholesome hours, as they are called, – would, I am convinced, in a medical point of view, prove the better caution. – That detestable picture, as I have said, gave the fashion to my dreams – if dreams they were – for the scene of them was invariably the room in which I lay. Had I never met with the picture, the fears would have come self-pictured in some shape or other –

Headless bear, black man, or ape –

but, as it was, my imaginations took that form. – It is not book, or picture, or the stories of foolish servants, which create these terrors in children. They can at most but give them a direction. Dear little T.H. [that is, Thornton Hunt, eldest son of the essayist Leigh Hunt] who of all children has been brought up with the most scrupulous exclusion of every taint of superstition – who was never allowed to hear of goblin or apparition, or scarcely to be told of bad men, or to read or hear of any distressing story – finds all this world of fear, from which he has been so rigidly excluded *ab extra*, in his own 'thick-coming fancies'; and from his little midnight pillow, this nurse-child of optimism will start at shapes, unborrowed of tradition, in sweats to which the reveries of the cell-damned murderer are tranquillity.

—'Witches, and other Night-Fears', *London Magazine*,
October 1821

When the bells justle in the tower
The hollow night amid
Then on my tongue the taste is sour
Of all I ever did.
—A. E. Housman (who is said to have
dreamed these lines)

֌ ֍

Shakespeare's Anachronistic Clocks

IACHIMO:

Swift, swift, you Dragons of the night, that dawning
May bear the Raven's eye: I lodge in feare
Though this a heavenly Angell, Hell is heere

[*Clock strikes.*]

One, two, three: time, time.

—*Cymbeline*, II.ii

Curious coincidence that the most famous of all Shakespeare's anachronistic striking clocks should also sound at 3 a.m., in *Julius Caesar*.

[*Clock strikes.*]

BRUTUS: Peace! Count the clock.
CASSIUS: The clock hath stricken three.

—*Julius Caesar*, II.i

֌ ֍

At 3.05 a.m. on the 22 June 1941, German artillery began to bombard
Russian positions – the opening salvo of Operation Barbarossa, Hitler's
invasion of the Soviet Union. It is the start of the greatest ground
offensive in recorded history: 138 German divisions against 148 Soviet
divisions.

Three of the clock

It is now the third hour, and the windows of heaven begin to open, and the sun begins to colour the clouds in the sky, before he shew his face to the world: now are the spirits of life, as it were, risen out of death: the cock calls the servants to their day's work, and the grass horses are fetched from their pastures; the milk-maids begin to look toward their dairy, and the good housewife begins to look about the house: the porridge pot is on for the servants' breakfast, and hungry stomachs will soon be ready for their victual: the sparrow begins to chirp about the house, and the birds in the bushes will bid them welcome to the field: the shepherd sets his pitch on the fire, and fills his tar-pot ready for his flock: the wheel and the reel begin to be set ready, and a merry song makes the work seem easy: the ploughman falls to harness his horses, and the thresher begins to look toward the barn: the scholar that loves learning will be hard at his book, and the labourer by great will be walking toward his work. In brief it is a parcel of time to good purpose, the exercise of nature and the entrance into art. Farewell.

—Nicholas Breton, *The Fantasticks*, 1626

ON THE LINNAEAN
FLORAL CLOCK

Linnaeus devised his plan for this clock at the University of Uppsala; it remains, as far as I know, the only means of telling the time by the sense of smell rather than sight, hearing or touch. He put a version of it into practice in the garden of his summer retreat at Hammerby (60 degrees north – so that the Goat's beard would indeed open at 3 a.m. to meet the first rays of the summer sun). A version only, since, alas, not all of the required species bloom at the same season.

Three of the morning
Goat's beard opens

Four of the morning
Chicory opens
Ox-tongue opens
Hawkbit (*Leontodon tuberosum*) opens

Five of the morning
Tawny Day-lily opens
Iceland Poppy opens
Common Sowthistle opens
Alpine Hawk's-beard opens
Dandelion opens

Six of the morning
Hawkweed (*Hieracium umbellatum*) opens
Cat's-ear opens

Seven of the morning
Madwort opens
Red Hawk's-beard opens
Wall Hawkbit opens
Felon Herb opens
Corn Sowthistle opens
St Bernard Lily opens
Cape Marigold opens
Hawkbit (*Leontodon hastile)* opens
White Waterlily opens
Lapland Sowthistle opens
Fig-Marigold (*Mesembryanthemum barbatum*) opens

Eight of the morning
Poor-Man's Weatherglass opens
Pink (*Dianthus prolifer*) opens

Auricula Hawkweed opens

Nine of the morning
Wayside Calendula opens   Dandelion closes
Chondrilla Hawkweed opens
Red Sand Spurry opens
Ice Plant opens   Goat's-beard closes

Ten of the Morning
Fig-Marigold (*Mesembryanthemum*   Chicory closes
nodiflourum*) opens

                                 Lettuce Flower closes
                                 Corn Sowthistle closes

Eleven of the morning   Alpine Hawk's-beard closes
                                 Common Sowthistle closes

At Noon   Wayside Calenddula closes
                                 Lapland Sowthistle closes

One of the evening   Pink (*Dianthus prolifer*) closes

Two of the evening   Fig-Marigold
                                 (*Mesembryanthemum
                                 barbatum*) closes
                                 Red Hawk's-beard closes
                                 Auricula Hawkweed closes

Three of the evening   Red Sand Spurry closes
                                 Ice plant closes
                                 Hawkbit (*Leontodon hastile*)
                                 closes
                                 Fig-Marigold
                                 (*Mesembryanthemum
                                 nodiflorum*) closes

Four of the evening	Cape Marigold closes
	Felon Herb closes
	Madwort closes
	St Bernard Lily closes
Five of the evening	
'Four-o'Clock' opens	Cat's-ear closes
	Hawkweed (*Hieracium*
	umbellatum) closes
	White Waterlily closes
Six of the evening	
Cranesbill (*Geranium triste)* opens	
Seven of the evening	Iceland Poppy closes
Eight of the evening	Tawny Day-lily closes
Nine of the evening	
Cactus grandiflorus opens	
Ten of the evening	
Night-flowering Catchfly opens	
At Midnight	*Cactus grandiflorus* closes

Botanists and gardeners of lower latitudes have also experimented with such floral clocks; at Innsbruck, Kerner von Marilaun planted a far more intricate version.

⊰ ⊱

'The Hour (or Time) of the Wolf': such is the usual English translation for the title of Ingmar Bergman's classic film, *Vargtimmen* (1967). Bergman's script defines the hour of the wolf as 'the time between midnight and dawn', but there is a substantial body of – mainly oral – popular lore that identifies it as the particularly grim sixty minutes (for the insomniac) between 3 and 4 a.m.

From *The Angel in the House,* by Coventry Patmore (1823– 96):

Going to Church

I woke at three; for I was bid
   To breakfast with the Dean at nine,
And thence to Church. My curtain slid,
   I found the dawning Sunday fine,
And could not rest, so rose. The air
   Was dark and sharp; the roosted birds
Cheep'd 'Here am I, Sweet; are you there?'
   On Avon's misty flats the herds
Expected, comfortless, the day,
   Which slowly fired the clouds above;
The cock scream'd, somewhere far away;
   In sleep the matrimonal dove
Was brooding; no wind waked the wood,
   Nor moved the midnight river-damps,
Nor thrill'd the poplar; quiet stood
   The chestnut with its thousand lamps;
The moon shone yet, but weak and drear,
   And seem'd to watch, with bated breath,
The landscape, all made sharp and clear,
   By stillness, as a face by death.

The action of James Lees-Milne's acerbic novella *Round the Clock* (1978), which follows the events in an English country house over the course of a single twenty-four-hour period, begins at 3 a.m. Each of its eight chapters concentrates on a major character, one canine, seven human, thus:

1. 3 a.m. to 6 a.m.: Nero (the dog)
2. 6 a.m. to 9 a.m.: Jasper (the family's younger son; Nero's master)
3. 9 a.m. to 12 noon: Adda (sexy 27-year-old wife of Jasper's older brother, 'Dolly')
4. 12 noon to 3 p.m. : Adolphus (the patriarch)
5. 3 p.m. to 6 p.m.: Emily (the 8-year old daughter of Adda and Dolly)
6. 6 p.m. to 9 p.m.: Lois (the matriarch)
7. 9 p.m. to 12 midnight: Dolly (feckless and lascivious)
8. 12. midnight to 3 a.m.: Mrs O'Grady (the housekeeper).

Most of the characters are plagued by impossible or inappropriate love: Jasper for Adda, Adda for Adolphus and so on. The tale does not have a happy ending.

Marcel Proust's Army Medical

Though Marcel Proust once replied to the question 'What event in military history do you admire most?' with the – flippant? nostalgic? faux-naif? – words 'My own enlistment as a volunteer', he had in fact dreaded the prospect of enlistment, and particularly the medical. Already a chronic insomniac, the young Marcel was sure that the hour of his medical would coincide with the one or two hours of daytime in which he was usually able to catch a little sleep. When his summons to the Invalides arrived, though, the time for his appointment was given as 3 a.m. Almost anyone else would have seen this as a simple misprint, or clerical error, but Marcel chose to interpret it as a heart-warming sign of how thoughtful the army could be to its recruits.

4 a.m. to 5 a.m.

Sad Steps

Groping back to bed after a piss
I part thick curtains, and am startled by
The rapid clouds, the moon's cleanliness.

Four o'clock: wedge-shadowed gardens lie
Under a cavernous, a wind-picked sky.
There's something laughable about this,

The way the moon dashes through clouds that blow
Loosely as cannon-smoke to stand apart
(Stone-coloured light sharpening the roofs below)

High and preposterous and separate –
Lozenge of love! Medallion of art!
O wolves of memory! Immensements! No,

One shivers slightly, looking up there.
The hardness and the brightness and the plain
Far-reaching singleness of that wide stare
Is a reminder of the strength and pain
Of being young; that it can't come again,
But is for others undiminished somewhere.
             —Philip Larkin, from *High Windows*, 1974

Larkin's title alludes to Sir Philip Sidney:

With how sad steps, O moon, thou climb'st the skies;
    How silently, and with how wan a face.

What, may it be that even in heav'nly place
That busy archer his sharp arrows tries?
Sure, if that long with love acquainted eyes
    Can judge of love, thou feel'st a lover's case;
    I read it in thy looks; thy languished grace
To me, that feel the like, thy state descries.
    Then even of fellowship, O moon, tell me,
Is constant love deemed there but want of wit?
Are beauties there as proud as here they be?
Do they above love to be loved, and yet
    Those lovers scorn whom that love doth possess?
    Do they call virtue there ungratefulness?
               —from *Astrophil and Stella*, 1581– 2

Sala Begins His Day-Long Pilgrimage Around London

Four o'clock in the morning. The deep bass voice of Paul's, the Staudigl of bells, has growlingly proclaimed the fact. Bow church confirms the information in a respectable baritone. St Clement Danes has sung forth acquiescence with the well-known chest-note of his tenor voice, sonorous and mellifluous as Tamberlick's. St Margaret's, Westminster, murmurs a confession of the soft impeachment with a contralto rich as Alboni's in 'Stridi la vampa;' and all around and about the pert bells of the new churches, from evangelical Hackney to Puseyite Pimlico, echo their announcement in shrill treble and soprani.

Four o'clock in the morning. Greenwich awards it, – the Horse Guards allow it – Bennett, arbiter of clocks that, with much striking, have grown blue in the face, has nothing to say against it. And that self-same hour shall never strike again this side the trumpet's sound. The hour itself being consigned to the innermost pigeon-hole of the Dead Hour office – (a melancholy charnel-house of misspent time is that, my friend) – you and I have close upon sixty minute before us ere the grim old scythe-bearer, the saturnine child-eater, who marks the seconds and minutes of which the infinite subdivision is a pulsation of eternity, will tell us that the term of another hour has come. That hour will be five a.m., and at five it is high market at Billingsgate. To that great piscatorial Bourse we, an't please you, are bound.

It is useless to disguise the fact that you, my shadowy, but not the less beloved companion, are about to keep very bad hours. Good to hear the chimes at midnight, as Justice Shallow and Falstaff oft did when they were students at Gray's Inn, but four and five in the morning! these be small hours indeed: this is beating the town with a vengeance. Were it winter, our bedlessness would be indefensible but this is still sweet summer time.

But why, the inquisitive may ask – the child-man who is for ever cutting up the bellows to discover the reservoir of the wind – why four a.m.? Why not begin our pilgrimage at one a.m., and finish the first half at midnight, in the orthodox get-up-and-go-to-bed manner? Simply because four a.m. is in reality the first hour of the working London day. The giant is wide awake at midnight; he sinks into a fitful slumber about two in the morning: short is his rest, for at four o'clock he is up again and at work, the busiest bee in the world's hive.

—George Augustus Sala, *Twice Around the Clock,* 1858– 9

Shadow

for Vita Milne

We stay up till gone four
in the morning
and another dawning
puts pay to moonwork.

While the rest of the street slept
here in your own back garden
you had your lover, that other self,
dropping to your feet

like an apple obeying
gravity's pull.

Our shadows are thrown longer
and thinner over the grass
until they reach the hedge
and a lattice-work of growth.

We examine it all: what's left
of the moon
and our shadows
standing up to fit us
like the perfect lover,

the bumps of the early fallers,
the dusty-furred crab apples
in their own indentations,
and again, behind trees,
the moon.

We see the possibilities.
—Peter Carpenter, *Choosing an*
England, 1997

John Milton's Working Day

He was an early riser (scil. At 4 a clock *mane*); yea, after he lost his
sight. He had a man to read to him. The first thing he read was
the Hebrew Bible, and that was at 4h. *mane*, $\frac{1}{2}$ h. +. Then he
contemplated.

At 7 his man came to him again, and then read to him again, and
wrote till dinner: the writing was as much as the reading. His
daughter, Deborah, could read to him Latin, Italian and French,
and Greeke …

After dinner he used to walk three or four hours at a time (he always had a garden where he lived); went to bed about 9.

—John Aubrey, *Brief Lives*, *c*.1680

Four in the Morning

At four this day of June I rise:
The dawn-light strengthens steadily;
Earth is a cerule mystery,
As if not far from Paradise
At four o'clock.

Or else near the Great Nebula,
Or where the Pleiads blink and smile:
(For though we see with eyes of guile
the grisly grin of things by day,
At four o'clock

They show their best.) ... In this vale's space
I am up the first, I think. Yet, no,
A whistling? And the to-and-fro
Wheezed whettings of a scythe apace
At four o'clock? ...

– Though pleasure spurred, I rose with irk:
Here is one at compulsion's whip
Taking his life's stern stewardship
With blithe uncare, and hard at work
At four o'clock!

—Thomas Hardy, 1925

⊰ ⊱

ON THE SYSTEM OF 'BELLS' AT SEA

0400 – or, in maritime reckoning, eight bells.

Before the advent of more exact technologies, the traditional system for telling time at sea was by the system of Ship's Bells. Every half hour, for a sequence of four times six hours, the ship's bell is rung one additional time in a series from one to eight. Thus, 12.30 is one bell, 1 a.m. is two bells, 1.30 is three bells ... and 4 a.m. is eight bells, at which point the sequence begins again, returning to eight bells at 8 a.m., noon, 4 p.m., 8 p.m. and midnight. (Time was measured by a sandglass.)

The system of bells overlaps but does not quite coincide with the division of the day into *watches*: the period in which a given number of the ship's company serve on deck. (Each group of men is also known as a watch. When the ship's company was divided into two, these were known as the larboard and starboard watches; when divided into three, they were usually known as the red, white, and blue watches.) The standard watches are:

Middle:	midnight to 0400
Morning:	0400 to 0800
Forenoon:	0800 to 1200
Afternoon:	1200 to 1600
First Dog:	1600 to 1800
Second (or Last) Dog:	1800 to 2000
First:	2000 to midnight.

The irregularity of the Dog watches is intended to make sure that the same men do not work the same watch each day.

Routine on board a warship was notoriously monotonous, and – except in cases of battle or calls at port – ran like this.

At around 0400, the Cook lit fires in the gallery and began to prepare breakfast – usually a disgusting mixture of oatmeal and sea-water known as 'burgoo' or 'skillagolee', washed down with so-called 'Ship's

Coffee', an equally unappealing beverage made of burned ship's biscuit boiled in water. Meanwhile, the Carpenter and Boatswain would come on deck to begin the day's repair work. At 0500 the crew would wash down the decks, polish the planks and perform other cleaning tasks. At about 0700 the First Lieutenant would come and check on this work, and at 0730 the Boastswain's Mate would pipe 'All hands, up hammocks', calling the rest of the ship's company on deck. At 0800 the Captain would come on deck, eight bells were struck and, at his discretion, the Boatswain would pipe breakfast.

At 0830 they would return to duty and the new watch would come on deck. Throughout the forenoon watch, many of the crew would work in 'messes' – groups based on their mess tables – and helped prepare the main meal of the day, served at 1200. The others would work on maintenance and repairs or, if off duty, sleep or relax. This routine might be interrupted at 1100, when the Captain might call all hands on deck to witness a punishment – a flogging. 'Dinner' – lunch – was served to all hands. The crew subsisted on biscuit, salt beef, pork with pea soup, cheese and the like, while the officers had more delicate and varied fare, including tea and sugar. From the year 1740 onwards, it became customary to issue a daily ration of a pint of grog, a mixture of rum and water; on voyages close to Britain or of less than a month's duration, the men might also receive a gallon a day of beer and a pint of wine.

At 1330, dinner done, the watch of deck would be called to duty; alternatively, the whole company would be required to take part in drills: fire drills, gunnery, sail handling and so on. A short evening meal was served at 1600, as the dog-watches changed. Just before sunset, a drummer would beat to quarters and all hands would report to battle stations for inspection by the officers.

At 2000, as the watch changed, all lights were extinguished so that the ship could not be seen from a distance, and the Master of Arms began his series of inspection rounds. The hours of darkness were punctuated by regular sentry reports of 'All's well'.

-ᴈ ᴇ-

Katherine Anne Porter, the American novelist, was woken one morning at 4 a.m. by the sound of her doorbell. It was her friend and fellow writer Elinor Wylie, who at that time was far wealthier and more successful then Porter, but was clearly in a state of some distress. 'I have stood the crassness of the world as long as I can,' she declared, 'and am going to kill myself. You are the only person in the world to whom I wish to say goodbye.' Sleepy and irritated, Porter replied, 'Elinor, it was very good of you to think of me. Goodbye.'

Four of the clock

It is now the fourth hour, and the sun begins to send her beams abroad, whose glimmering brightness no eye can behold: now crows the cock lustily and claps his wings for joy of the light, and with his hens leaps lightful from his roost: now are the horses at their chaff and provender, the servants at breakfast, the milk-maid gone to the field, and the spinner at the wheel; and the shepherd with his dog are going toward the fold: now the beggars rouse them out of the hedges, and begin their morning craft; but if the constable come, beware the stocks: the birds now begin to flock, and the sparhawk begins to prey for his aerie; the thresher begins to stretch his long arms, and the thriving labourer will fall hard to his work: the quick-witted brain will be quoting of places, and the cunning workman will be trying of his skill: the hounds begin to be coupled for the chase, and the spaniels follow the falconer to the field; travellers begin to look toward the stable, where an honest hostler is worthy his reward: the soldier now is upon discharge of his watch, and the captain with his company may take as good rest as they can. In sum, I thus conclude of it: I hold it the messenger of action and the watch of reason. Farewell.
—Nicholas Breton, *The Fantasticks*, 1626

At 4.45 a.m. on 1 September 1939, five German armies of fifty-eight divisions (including Panzers) inaugurated the 'Blitzkrieg' mode of war by invading Poland, and thus precipitating the Second World War.

⊰ ⊱

5 a.m. to 6 a.m.

The Times

05:00 hours is bad and anything with a three in it,
for example 03:13. Those times between 02:00 and 04:00
are crippling for the next day's decisions as are those times
on a Sunday and most times during the ravages of February.
Unspeakable times include 04:59 and 01:07 – but for some reason
05:58 is not a bad time, unlike its cousins 01:58 and 02:58
who are total buggers and always will be. Among the joke-times
are anything before midnight, the lucid moments just after midnight
and those just after making love, with sleep approaching.

The why-even-bother-times are as follows: 06:14, 06:27, 06:32
and the infrequently mentioned 06:02. The I-want-to-die-now-times
list 02:09, 04:11 and 03.33. The fact we all go on living regardless
must point to something, the resilience of the human spirit, perhaps,
equality of opportunity for fathers, or even Japanese alarm clock reliability.
However, my familiarity with 04:19 of late has wrenched the bottom
drawer from my desk and scattered the contents blowing across the park
to be laughed at by children and dogs. I find this is inducing in me
a quite serious indifference to most subjects, even my work.
—Anthony Wilson, *Nowhere Better Than This,* 2002

Arnold Auerbach, the baseball manager, was once on tour with the Boston Celtics. At five o'clock one morning, he ran into three of his players, each with an attractive young woman on his arm. To gloss over the tricky situation – the men were supposed to be observing a strict sleep regime – one of the men introduced his lady friend as a 'cousin'. Auerbach, willing to let the fiction pass, nodded politely, until the flustered man went on to explain that they were all on their way to an early church service. 'I fined him twenty-five dollars for insulting my intelligence,' Auerbach reported.

In similar vein:

When he was a student, the American footballer Robert 'Tiny' Maxwell (d. 1922), who throughout his life was the target of jokes about his stuttering, once got permission to travel to a nearby town one night, provided that he return by 1 a.m. at the latest. When he finally got back, his irate coach demanded of him what time it was.

'A little before wuh-wuh-one,' stuttered Maxwell.

The college clock struck five.

'Either you're a liar,' snarled the coach, 'or that clock stutters as badly as you do.'

-ᘯ ᘰ-

ON EARLY RISING

In winter, at five o'clock, servant arise,
In summer at four, is very good guise.
—*Five Hundred Points of Good Husbandry*,
Thomas Tusser, 1571

Advice from Benjamin Franklin:

'He that would thrive must rise at five.' The poor can ill afford to lose two or three hours of the best portion of the day. Economy of time and diligence in business, are virtues peculiarly appropriate to those who depend upon their earnings for the means of

subsistence. Allow twelve working hours to a day, he who by rising at eight instead of five o'clock in the morning, thereby loses three hours' labor daily, parts with one-fourth of his means of supporting himself, and family: ten years' labour lost in the course of forty years!
—from *Poor Richard's Almanac*; reprinted in the
Southern Farmer, January 1851

Franklin practised what he preached. Here is his account of a typical day:

5 – 8 a.m. Rise, wash, and address Powerful Goodness; contrive Day's Business and take the Resolution of the Day; prosecute the present study; and breakfast? –

8 – 12 a.m. Work.

12 – 2 p.m. Read, or overlook my Accounts, and dine.

2 – 6 p.m. Work.

6 – 9 p.m. Put Things in their Places, Supper, Musick, or Diversion, or Conversation, Examination of the Day.

9 p.m. – 5 a.m. Sleep.
—'Scheme for Employment for the Twenty-Four Hours of a natural Day', in *The Autobiography*, 1771– 90

Rise at 5; counting-house till 8; then breakfast on toast and Cheshire cheese; in his shop for two hours, then a neighbouring coffee house for news; shop again, till dinner at home at 12 on a 'thundering joint'; 1 o'clock on Change; 3, Lloyd's Coffee House for business; shop again for an hour; then another coffee house for recreation, followed by 'sack shop' to drink with acquaintances, till home for a 'light supper' and so to bed 'before Bow Bell rings 9.

—Ned Ward, *The Wealthy Shopkeeper*, 1706

We had to be up at 5 in the morning to get to the factory, ready to begin work at 6, then work while 8, when we stopped $\frac{1}{2}$ an hour for breakfast, then work to 12 noon; for dinner we had 1 hour, then work while 4. We then had $\frac{1}{2}$ an hour for tee, and tee if anything was left, then commenced work again on to 8.30. Then we went to what was called home. Many times I have been asleep when I had taken my last spoon of porridge – not even washed, we were so overworked and underfed. I used to curse the road we walked on ...

> —An account by the Yorkshireman George Oldfield
> of his working life at the age of nine, *c*.1842

(Oldfield wrote this memoir as an old man, in 1904; it was published in The Hungry Forties: Life under the Bread Tax, 1904.)

The poet Robert Southey (1744– 1843) regularly rose at five and liked to boast of the fact. On meeting a Quaker lady, he proudly informed her that he rose at five, read Spanish from six to eight, read French from eight to nine, wrote poetry from nine to eleven, wrote prose from eleven to one, and so on until bedtime. The lady heard him out, then said 'And pray, Friend, when dost thou think?'

The operative must be in the mill at half-past five in the morning; if he comes a couple of minutes too late, he is fined; if he comes ten minutes too late, he is not let in until breakfast is over, and a quarter of the day's wages is withheld, though he loses only two and one-half hours' work out of twelve. He must eat, drink, and sleep at command. For satisfying the most imperative needs, he is vouchsafed the least possible time absolutely required by them. Whether his dwelling is a half-hour or a whole one removed from the factory does not concern his employer. The despotic bell calls him from his bed, his breakfast, his dinner.

> —Friedrich Engels, *The Condition of the Working Class*
> *in England*, 1845 (trans. Florence Kelley-
> Wischnewetsky, 1887)

It was my practice to be at my table every morning at 5.30 am, and it was also my practice to show myself no mercy ... It had at this time become my custom ... to write with my watch before me, and to require from myself 250 words every quarter of an hour. I have found that the 250 words have been as forthcoming as regularly as my watch went.

—Anthony Trollope, *An Autobiography*, 1883

I wake as a matter of course, about half past five, and get up and go out on my balcony in my nightgown to see if there's going to be a nice dawn ... Generally there is a good dawn ... At six I get up, and dress, with occasional balcony interludes – but always get to my writing table at seven, where, by scolding and paying, I secure my punctual cup of coffee, and do a bit of the *Laws of Plato* to build my day on. I find Jowett's translation is good for nothing and shall do one myself, as I've intended these fifteen years. At half past seven the gondola is waiting and takes me to the bridge before St John and Paul, where I give an hour of my very best day's work to painting the school of Mark and vista of Canal to Murano. It's a great Canaletto view, and I'm painting it against him.

I am rowed back to breakfast at nine, and, till half past ten, think over and write what little I can of my new fourth vol. of *Stones of Venice*. At half past ten, I go to the Academy, where I find Moore at work; and we sit down to our picture together. They have been very good to me in the Academy, and have taken down St Ursula and given her to me all to myself in a locked room and perfect light. I'm painting a small carefully toned general copy of it for Oxford, and shall make a little note of it for you, and am drawing various parts larger. Moore is making a study of the head, which promises to be excellent.

He sits beside me till twelve, then goes to early dinner with Mrs Moore and Bessie – I have a couple of hours *tête-à-tête* with St Ursula, very good for me. I strike work at two or a little after – go home, read letters, and dine at three. Lie on sofa and read any vicious book I can to amuse me – to prevent St Ursula having it all her own way. Am greatly amused with the life of Casanova at present. At half-past-four, gondola again, – I am floated, half asleep, to Murano – or the Armenians – or the San Giorgio in Alga – wake up, and make some little evening sketch, by way of diary. Then take oar myself, and row into the dark or moonlight. Home at seven, well heated – quiet tea – after that, give audiences, if people want me; otherwise read Venetian history – if no imperative letters – and to bed at ten.'

  —John Ruskin to Charles Eliot Norton, 5 October 1876

'This is the day that the Lord hath made; let us rejoice and be glad in it.' Rose before six to prayer and meditation. Ah, blessed God, how many in the mills and factories have risen at four, on this day even, to toil and suffering!

  —The Journal of Lord Shaftesbury, Christmas Day 1843
    (from *The Life and Work of the Seventh Earl of Shaftesbury*, by Edwin Hodder, 1888)

-≼ ≽-

In Harmony, the Utopian community of Charles Fourier (1772–1837), the first meal of the day – the Matutinal – was served at 5 a.m. It was followed by lunch at 8 a.m., dinner at 1 p.m., a snack at 6 p.m., and supper at 9 p.m., eked out by two collations at 10 a.m. and 4 p.m.

'The darkest hour is just before the dawn', runs the old saying – usually with the cheerful implication that we should gird our loins in the expectation that extreme misery will soon be relieved. T. S. Eliot, never one to go in much for complacency or breezy optimism, thought of this hour as something altogether more ambiguous: who knows what the coming of light might display to us? Hence, in 'Little Gidding', his phrase 'In the uncertain hour before the morning ...' As the critic Christopher Ricks has pointed out, modern English contains a few well-known words for the gloom that follows day – 'twilight', 'gloaming', 'dusk' (which even Eliot is driven to use for his poem) – but the precise, or pedantic word for the gloom before dawn is rare and archaic: 'antelucan'.

Five of the clock

It is now five of the clock, and the sun is going apace upon his journey; and fie sluggards who would be asleep: the bells ring to prayer, and the streets are full of people, and the highways are stored with travellers: the scholars are up and going to school, and the rods are ready for the truants' correction: the maids are at milking, and the servants at plough, and the wheel goes merrily, while the mistress is by: the capons and the chickens must be served without door, and the hogs cry till they have their swill: the shepherd is almost gotten to his fold, and the herd begins to blow his horn through the town: the blind fiddler is up with his dance and his song, and the alehouse door is unlocked for good fellows; the hounds begin to find after the hare, and horse and foot follow after the cry; the traveller now is well on his way, and if the weather be fair, he walks with the better cheer: the carter merrily whistles to his horse, and the boy with his sling casts stones at the crows; the lawyer now begins to look on his case, and if he give good counsel, he is worthy of the fee. In brief, not to stay too long upon it, I hold it the necessity of labour and the note of profit. Farewell.

—Nicholas Breton, *The Fantasticks*, 1626

MARCELLUS:
It faded on the crowing of the cock.
Some say, that ever 'gainst that season comes
Wherein our Saviour's birth is celebrated,
The bird of dawning singeth all night long:
And then (they say) no spirit can walk abroad,
The nights are wholesome, then no planets strike,

No fairy takes, nor witch hath power to charm:
So hallow'd, and so gracious is the time.

HORATIO:
So have I heard, and do in part believe it.
But look, the morn in russet mantle clad
Walks o'er the dew of yon high eastern hill ...
—*Hamlet*, I.i

The Piper at the Gates of Dawn

Then suddenly the Mole felt a great Awe fall upon him, an awe that turned his muscles to water, bowed his head, and rooted his feet to the ground. It was no panic terror – indeed he felt wonderfully at peace and happy – but it was an awe that smote and held him, and, without seeing, he knew it could only mean that some august Presence was very, very near. With difficulty he turned to look for his friend, and saw him at his side cowed, stricken, and trembling violently. And still there was utter silence in the populous bird-haunted branches around them; and still the light grew and grew.

Perhaps he would never have dared to raise his eyes, but that, though the piping was now hushed, the call and the summons seemed still dominant and imperious. He might not refuse, were Death himself waiting to strike him instantly, once he had looked with mortal eye on things rightly kept hidden. Trembling he obeyed, and raised his humble head; and then, in that utter clearness of the imminent dawn, while Nature, flushed with fullness of incredible colour, seemed to hold her breath for the event, he looked in the very eyes of the Friend and Helper; saw the backward sweep of the curved horns gleaming in the growing daylight; saw the stern, hooked nose between the kindly eyes that were looking down on them humorously, while the bearded mouth broke into a half-smile at the corners; saw the rippling muscles on the arm that lay across the broad chest, the long supple hand still holding the pan-pipes only just fallen away from the parted lips; saw the splendid curves of the shaggy limbs disposed in majestic ease on the sward; saw, last of all, nestling between his very hooves, sleeping soundly in entire peace and contentment, the little, round, podgy, childish form of the baby otter. All this he saw, for one moment breathless and intense, vivid on the morning sky; and still, as he looked, he lived; and still, as he lived, he wondered.

'Rat!' he found breath to whisper, shaking. 'Are you afraid?'

'Afraid?' murmured the Rat, his eyes shining with unutterable love. 'Afraid! Of *Him*? O, never, never! And yet – and yet – O, Mole, I am afraid!'

Then the two animals, crouching to the earth, bowed their heads and did worship.

Sudden and magnificent, the sun's broad golden disc showed itself over the horizon facing them; and the first rays, shooting across the level water-meadows, took the animals full in the eyes and dazzled them. When they were able to look once more, the Vision had vanished, and the air was full of the carol of birds that hailed the dawn.

—Kenneth Grahame, *The Wind in the Willows*, 1908